'As I read this book, each page left me feeling more em-powered than the last. Shedding light on many forgotten scriptural accounts of fearless women whom God raised up, Elaine succinctly gathers their stories and opens our eyes to the high places they occupied. She gives us hope for a brighter future – reminding us that we are to continue the legacy of these heroines, and even points us to organizations already deployed on the front lines.'
Ruth Akinradewo, Press Red Ambassador, author and social justice activist

'This book blows wide open the all-too-common assumption that women in the Bible always bowed to a patriarchal system. Elaine Storkey brings their stories vividly to life, then paral-lels their experience and wisdom with events and initiatives today – enabling us to respond to contemporary challenges with informed understanding of the revolutionary roles that many women played in biblical times. I was inspired, espe-cially by how Jesus affirmed the value and significance of the women he met, whatever their position in society, and how female disciples were pivotal to the life of the early Church.'
Julia Bicknell, former BBC journalist for *Woman's Hour*, first *Breakfast* host, Premier Radio, and co-founder of <WorldWatchMonitor.org>

'In Elaine Storkey's wise, compassionate and scholarly hands these familiar stories erupt like gentle fireworks bringing fresh illumination, excitement, colour and impact. Wonderfully in-spiring and thought-provoking.'
Henrietta Blyth, Chief Executive Officer, Open Doors UK and Ireland

D1580615

'Elaine Storkey tells a brilliant story, weaving the lives of outstanding biblical role models with informed commentary on current affairs, and highlighting ways in which women can resist being victims of the system. Her book is easy to read yet full of profound wisdom, encouraging all of us to take what we have and use it for God's glory. None of us is insignificant and none of us is powerless. We just have to use what we have with courage.'
Bev Murrill, speaker, author and director

'Elaine Storkey is well known as a perceptive writer, speaker and broadcaster on contemporary theological, social and ethical issues. In this new volume, she brings her deep scholarship and wide experience to tell the stories of some of the women found in the Bible, including many of the lesser-known characters. As well as bringing to life the historical realities of these women, she also draws parallels between their lives and ours, challenging us to act with the same boldness, courage, wisdom, integrity and intelligence. Storkey's insight into the lives of these women is augmented by her immense knowledge of the challenges of women's lives across the globe today. As in everything she writes, this book combines rigour with deep humanity and faith, inspiring and challenging us to enlarge our understanding of God and of our own potential to engage with and shape the world around us.'
Christina Rees CBE, writer, broadcaster and former chair of National WATCH (Women and the Church)

'This immersive, persuasive and triumphant celebration of women is smart, bold and brave, cheering us on and challenging us to live lives of liberation. Faith and ethics dance effortlessly together, as biblical women look us firmly in the eye.'
Rachie Ross, eco-theologian

Elaine Storkey is a philosopher, sociologist and theologian who has held university posts at King's College, London; Stirling; Oxford; Calvin College, USA; and the Open University. A Fellow of Aberystwyth University, high-table member of Newnham College, Cambridge, and former Director of the London Institute for Contemporary Christianity, she has also lectured in Africa, Asia, Canada and Haiti. Her presidency of Tearfund, the aid and development agency, spanned 17 years. A broadcaster and author, she has been a passionate advocate for justice and gender issues for 30 years, implementing many changes for women through 28 years on the General Synod of the Church of England. Her writings include *The Search for Intimacy* (Hodder/Eerdmans, 1994) and *The Origins of Difference* (Baker, 2002). Her most recent book, *Scars Across Humanity: Understanding and overcoming violence against women* (SPCK, 2015/IVP USA, 2018), won the *Christianity Today* 2019 Book of the Year Award, Politics and Public Life.

WOMEN IN A PATRIARCHAL WORLD

Twenty-five empowering
stories from the Bible

Elaine Storkey

First published in Great Britain in 2020

Society for Promoting Christian Knowledge
36 Causton Street
London SW1P 4ST
www.spck.org.uk

Copyright © Elaine Storkey 2020

All rights reserved. No part of this book may be reproduced or
transmitted in any form or by any means, electronic or mechanical,
including photocopying, recording, or by any information storage and
retrieval system, without permission in writing from the publisher.

SPCK does not necessarily endorse the individual
views contained in its publications.

Scripture quotations are taken from the NIV or the NRSV.

The Holy Bible, New International Version (Anglicized edition) is
copyright © 1979, 1984, 2011 by Biblica. Used by permission of Hodder
& Stoughton Ltd, an Hachette UK company. All rights reserved. 'NIV'
is a registered trademark of Biblica. UK trademark number 1448790.

The New Revised Standard Version of the Bible, Anglicized
Edition, is copyright © 1989, 1995 by the Division of Christian
Education of the National Council of the Churches of Christ
in the USA. Used by permission. All rights reserved.

British Library Cataloguing-in-Publication Data
A catalogue record for this book is available from the British Library

ISBN 978–0–281–08407–4
eBook ISBN 978–0–281–08408–1

1 3 5 7 9 10 8 6 4 2

Typeset by Falcon Oast Graphic Art Ltd

First printed in Great Britain by Jellyfish Print Solutions
Subsequently digitally printed in Great Britain

eBook by Falcon Oast Graphic Art Ltd

Produced on paper from sustainable forests

To

Iona Ella Storkey,
along with her cousins and brother:
Zadok, Torin, Kieran, Elijah and Ezekiel

Contents

Contents

Acknowledgements

Some of the chapters in this book are based on articles that first saw the light of day in the magazine *Woman Alive*. I wrote them in a much shorter form, encouraged by the stalwart editor, Jackie Harris, who worked hard to bring a stimulating monthly journal to women of faith. I want to express my thanks here for all her encouragement and sisterhood in a number of projects.

I'm grateful too to a number of people who have worked in biblical studies themselves and provided the resources for others. My friend Cathy Kroeger would have been delighted to read all that is being done in these areas since her death. And I want to acknowledge women from backgrounds other than my own who continue to open up the Bible for other women across the world: Rosalee Velloso Ewell, Ruth Padilla DeBorst, Melba Maggay, Faith Forster, Kate Coleman, Cham Kaur-Mann, Bev Murrill, Lauran Bethel, Ann-Marie Isenring, Joy Graetz, Jen Singh, Tarana Mirzoyeva, Katei Kirby and so many others – it has been a privilege to work with you.

I'm grateful to the library at Newnham College, Cambridge, for providing resources for me, and to those, like Anne Roberts, who suggested amendments to the text. I am also indebted again to the editorial team at SPCK for their professionalism. But as ever, my ongoing thanks go to Alan, who is never happier than when we reach the end of a project and are able to share the results of our work with others.

Introduction

Storytelling is a powerful form of communication. At the very least, it presents us with characters, a location and a plot and invites us to listen in. Good storytelling goes much further. It opens up the shared humanity of others so that we can get inside their life situations, travel with them and learn from their experiences.

Much of traditional Christian teaching involves us in understanding doctrine. This is important, because people who embrace the Christian faith need to reflect on the teachings and creeds that form the contours of their beliefs, and know what they are giving assent to. We think of doctrine as contained in the Torah, the wisdom of the Prophets, the teachings of Jesus in the Gospels, and the letters to the early Church by St Paul and others. Yet we should not underestimate the part played by narrative theology in both framing our doctrine and shaping our understanding of faith. The stories of people in Scripture are case histories of God's relationship with human-kind. They are not fables, not other-worldly myths and legends. They concern the experiences of folk like us. The stories may go back centuries and be located in very different cultures, but they remain the stuff that our human lives are made of. The same joys and fears, struggles and decisions, sin and redemption speak into our own existence, often in ways that take us by surprise.

This book looks at stories about women. In doing so,

we need to acknowledge that much of biblical literature is written by men. Consequently, some feminist writers have developed a 'hermeneutic of suspicion', identifying the patriarchal context of the biblical text and questioning whether it can ever properly present women's authentic lives and experiences. My own approach accepts the question, but suggests that a hermeneutic of suspicion needs to work alongside a hermeneutic of faith, so the stories can be read in as full a way as possible. For the Bible is full of women's stories. Frequently, the men are the ones depicted badly by the storyteller. In other stories, men barely feature at all, except in the background or as powerful outsiders. So, though the scribes might be male, and the context reflect a patriarchal culture where male voices predominate, I believe many stories are authentically those of women. I believe, too, that the original sources for the stories will have been the women themselves.

In retelling some of those women's stories this volume is selective. It does not include every woman who is part of a biblical narrative, but focuses specifically on those who faced challenges and had crucial decisions to make. My retelling invites you to join me to explore the authenticity of their accounts; to find, despite the gap of time, an echo of our lives in their narratives. Even more than that, I believe that we can learn today from those challenges they faced so many centuries ago, and become stronger ourselves. Before you read my own text, I invite you to read the Bible passage at the heading of each story and reflect on it yourself. When you pool your reflections with mine, we might find that, together, our insights make us richer.

Because it puts us in touch with the living God, Scripture is alive in many ways. And one of those ways is its ability to take our human stories and point us back to the very source and meaning of our being. If this book succeeds in drawing you a little closer to the love of God and the way God can empower your own life more deeply, I shall be more than satisfied.

1

Call the midwives!

EXODUS 1.5–22

Just imagine you're a midwife, committed to helping women through a safe labour and delivering a healthy baby. It's a job you love, and it gives you great satisfaction to be there at the beginnings of new life. Then, an unexpected order comes down from the highest political authorities that all midwives have to practise selective abortion. Close to the end of the birth process, and as soon as the genitals are identified, you must eliminate all babies of the 'wrong' sex and 'wrong' ethnicity. No choice of conscience is offered; no mediating circumstance. And the penalty for disobeying the order is likely to be severe: it could be disqualification, imprisonment or possibly even death. You stare at the document that has been delivered personally to you; your name is on the order. You have no friends in high places who can advise you. How would you respond?

This was exactly the dilemma faced by Shiphrah and Puah, two Hebrew midwives in Exodus 1. They were part of the huge Jewish population living in Egypt. By this period, the fertility rate among the Hebrew women was high, and the two midwives had their hands full – of babies! The edict from on high must have come as a very unpleasant shock.

With new mums already going into labour, however were they going to respond?

There is, of course, much background to this story. The Jewish presence in Egypt had started with Joseph, hundreds of years before. Joseph had been sold into slavery by his brothers, but ended up as a key official in Pharaoh's Egyptian court because of his spiritual discernment of dreams. When he foretold of an impending long famine, Pharaoh gave him the job of implementing his clear, far-sighted policies for coping with it. The confidence of Pharaoh was justified, for Joseph effectively saved Egypt's population from starvation. Yet famine rapidly spread elsewhere, and Joseph's family came to Egypt for food, to be followed by many more from Canaan. The Israelites stayed, grew in number and settled down as permanent residents of Egypt.

Now, hundreds of years later, Joseph had been long forgotten and a harsh regime saw the size of the immigrant Jewish population as a threat. The current pharaoh (possibly Ramesses II) looked over his shoulder to Egypt's many enemies beyond their borders, and feared the Israelites might eventually form some alliance with others against him. So he began to curtail their effectiveness. He forced them into slave labour, putting them under brutal taskmasters, weakening their spirits and making their lives a general misery. Oppression followed oppression. But still the Hebrew people multiplied. Still the midwives were kept busy!

Pharaoh then stepped back and decided on a more drastic remedy. It seemed an obvious one. Cut down the birth rate of this growing ethnic minority in Egypt. In particular, he decided on the elimination of boy babies. They could allow the girls to live – they were always useful as wives or concubines for the Egyptians, but boys would provide a potential fighting force for the Israelites. A cull of male babies before they even took their first breath would ensure that the whole population would eventually dwindle and the threat be removed. The order was thus given to instruct all midwives that Hebrew boys were not to be born.

Shiphrah and Puah may not have been expecting this, and would not have known who to turn to for advice. They had no political or economic power. They were not wealthy or well connected in professional hierarchies. They simply helped other Jewish women give birth. Effectively, they were in a subservient position to a subservient people. Despite all this, they showed no sign of being cowed by the edict. They had minds of their own. They also had strong beliefs and values, which stemmed from their Jewish faith. The story tells us that they 'feared God' more than they feared the king of Egypt (and 'fear' here means 'reverence' rather than 'dread'). It was this fear and their own moral fibre that enabled them to enter into what was effectively a high-stakes power play with the king of the ruling nation! They simply ignored the order.

Doing nothing is certainly one way of facing a challenge. We often do that when we are out of our depth or can't think what else to do. It can be a very passive response and some- times just multiplies the problem. That was not the case here. By ignoring the order, the midwives were responding with a powerful act of supreme rebellion. They rejected the king's authority and continued with the professional (and spiritual) values of their own calling. Their refusal to obey wasn't at all passive. It was a deliberate stand against illegitimate orders, and Shiphrah and Puah knew the risk. They were stepping out in the same kind of principled conviction that has been echoed by martyrs throughout the ages.

It was not a stand that would go unnoticed for long, however. When there was clearly no change in the frequency of male births in that area, the pharaoh sent a summons to the midwives and demanded to know why they had allowed the boys to live. Their response could certainly be seen as something of an insult to the king's intelligence: 'Hebrew women are so much more vigorous than Egyptian women; by the time we arrive, the babies are already born.' At the very least, this reply must have left the king perplexed. Obviously, he was no authority on the gynaecology of Hebrew women, but he must have had his suspicions. It was a very high-risk strategy by the midwives. Nevertheless it paid off. They were not arrested, prosecuted or imprisoned. Not only did they get away with their defiance of the pharaoh, their lives were blessed abundantly by God. Because they insisted on choosing life rather than death for their people, Shiphrah and Puah's bravery was vindicated. They were given very special gifts of new life, in families of their own.

The midwives were protected and received no punishment, but we know that the pharaoh did not give up. Tyrants rarely do. His next policy was infanticide. Many deaths were to occur. Blood would be shed. And more women would be called on for further defiance. But the initial challenge had been faced by these faithful midwives. The pattern of defying tyrannical authority had been set. The part played by Shiphrah and Puah as liberationists remained significant in Israel's history and is even implicitly acknowledged in the Talmud: 'It was the reward of the righteous women of that generation that caused Israel to be redeemed from Egypt.' Christians can follow suit and echo their own appreciation for these spunky women.

Facing our challenges today

This story speaks into a number of areas of our lives today. Issues about life and death come into every period in history. Today, the morality of abortion is still being debated across the world, with ethical advocates speaking loudly on each side. In one direction, states that have accepted abortion laws are rescinding them, making abortion a criminal offence. In the other direction, those who speak out against the ethics of abortion can find their nursing or medical careers curtailed. Pro-choice and pro-life campaigners both often have blind spots. 'Pro-choice' people have little time for those whose choice is against abortion, and 'pro-life' people are often adamantly opposed to other pro-life measures, like gun control.

Caught up in the middle are many women struggling with personal decisions about abortion. Shiphrah and Puah's story encourages them to have the courage to think and pray the issues through before God, and not be driven by pressure from others or by prevailing cultural values. It encourages Christian doctors and nurses today, who often have to make difficult choices in relation to the beginnings of life. It says we have to allow both deep compassion for those women who face the challenge of an unwanted pregnancy and freedom of conscience regarding the right to life of a viable foetus.

In non-Western cultures there are other resonances with this story today, not least the incidence of sex-selective abortion and infanticide rampant in India and other Asian countries. This time, the sex discrimination is reversed. Few celebrations follow the birth of a daughter, and many Indian mothers face the difficult challenge of what to do if they are pregnant with a girl in a culture where boys are of greater significance and value, and also command the dowry. There is often enormous pressure on the mother to abort. Issues of both poverty and affluence combine to produce a huge distortion in the gender ratio in India's population and put many girls' lives at risk.

Yet, here too, like those Hebrew midwives, brave cam-paigners in India, especially midwives, doctors and mothers, defy the prevailing ideologies and work to change the cultural climate. They take their own stand, naming those who profit from the selective abortion industry and calling authorities to account in not bringing violators to justice. Facing any of these challenges brings its own risks: campaigners can be attacked or murdered, mothers refusing abortions can be tortured by in-laws, or even 'disappear'. The challenge for us as Christians is to stand alongside those who work for what is right, and pray for cultural change across the world so that each sex is valued equally.

Yet the story of Shiphrah and Puah has relevance beyond the abortion issue. It speaks into any area of injustice. It encourages all of us to stand up for what is right in any cultural climate hostile to principled living before God. It speaks to those women who have embraced pacifism in times of conflict and given themselves to working for peace. It helps us face the challenge of social action, whether related to health, work, poverty, age or gender. It can guide us to help defend those who have no voice, and who are therefore easily overlooked or exploited in our materialist age. It can draw us to stand alongside other people who are penalized for their stand and support them. And it can challenge us to refuse to be part of the silent majority, who look on while wrongdoing becomes a way of life.

The two midwives were called by God to respond in the place where they belonged. It is the same for us. The challenges that many of us face are local but nonetheless demanding. They exist within our place of work, our family and our neighbourhood. Enough issues exist in any of these areas to keep all of us busy! Our starting point is prayer for discernment, persistence and courage. And if we are reaching out to those who are lonely, bereaved, frustrated or broken, the challenge is to be there for others and bring hope into their lives. Like Shiphrah and Puah, we might be called to take on principalities and powers. But like them also, we need to recognize that we do nothing on our own. For God is with us and will work through us.

Questions to ponder

1 Why do you think that midwives were given so much autonomy in traditional societies?
2 What do you think can bring change in those societies today where girl babies are aborted because of their sex?

2

A calm mother, a sharp sister and a wet princess

EXODUS 2.1–10

No one ever forgets the story of Moses in the bulrushes. It was certainly a favourite Bible story for me as a girl. The narrative has travelled through history and is echoed today even in our consumerist culture. Browsing an online catalogue I read, 'If you want to keep your newborn baby safe and secure, there is nothing better than this lovely Moses basket.' I smiled, however, as I looked at the picture. The white wicker cradle, draped in gleaming white fleece, would not have offered much protection to the original Moses!

The historical story is brutal and terrifying. With no reduction in the childbirth ratio among the Hebrews, despite his edicts, the pharaoh adopted a new approach. He would go for annihilation. Infanticide would be an effective method of eliminating the Israelites' next generation. So the pharaoh ordered a cull where newborn Hebrew boys would be thrown into the Nile. One of the babies in enormous danger was Moses.

In this story in Exodus, the lives of three women were interwoven in an extraordinary way. Each one faced the same challenge, but from a different perspective. The challenge was simple: how to keep the baby Moses from being killed or drowned in the river. But the task was formidable. The Egyptians soldiers were combing systematically through the homes of the Hebrews and seizing any baby boys they found. Newborn infants could not be hidden for long. Sooner or later, each male offspring would be found and murdered.

Moses' mother, Jochebed, faced the challenge first. She had just given birth to a healthy son. She had older children also, Aaron and Miriam, but they were out of danger, because the pharaoh's order was for infanticide not full-scale child sacrifice. We can only imagine the terror that must have plagued that mother night and day, waiting for the soldiers to come and take her precious infant. As she heard the sobbing of her neighbours and the screams of anguished mothers, she knew it was only a matter of time. Unless God somehow prevented his murder, there was no hope.

When Jochebed could no longer hide the baby at home, she came up with an audacious plan. Why not try to hide him in the river itself? With the bodies of dead offspring in abundance, a live one might not be noticed. So with as little publicity as possible, she made a cradle of papyrus and river plants, carefully disguising it to look like natural vegetation. She waterproofed it with slime and pitch until it was a safe vessel for her beloved son. Then, cradle and baby were sent floating gently to the bulrushes by the edge of the River Nile, no doubt covered with prayers for a safe outcome. Satisfied that she could do no more, the mother dispatched his older sister to keep watch at a careful distance.

The challenge of keeping the baby safe was now faced by Miriam. It was a huge responsibility for a young girl, the kind of life-and-death challenge that children should never have to face. Yet, unlike her mother, she would not be under suspicion if she hung around the river. Youngsters often played there, paddling or swimming when the heat was oppressive. We can picture her, surreptitiously creeping to the reeds, reassuring her baby brother, giving the child water, or maybe even milk that her mother had expressed. Several trips in and out of the water would raise no questions. This could not go on for long, however. Even with extreme caution, a river is no place for long-term childcare! We can only assume that both Jochebed and Miriam were praying that God would provide a way for their baby to be rescued and put out of danger.

Miriam's watch was interrupted by the third woman to face the challenge: Pharaoh's daughter, Bithia. She had come with her handmaidens down to the river to bathe. Bathing time would almost certainly have been regulated to the period when the river was free from drowning babies. We cannot believe that Pharaoh would want his daughter to be exposed to such carnage. Perhaps the soldiers came to remove bodies, or send them down the Nile, far away from where Bithia might swim. Whatever the process, the princess and her handmaidens were splashing contentedly when something floating among the bulrushes caught their attention. Sending one of her handmaidens, she was presented with a well-concealed basket, in which a three-month-old baby was very much alive and needing attention.

It is easy to reflect on what would have been going

through Miriam's mind as she watched the servant present her brother to this elegant, rich young mistress. Would the Egyptian princess call the guards? Would she hurl him into the river herself? For it was obvious that he was a Hebrew boy. Miriam must have felt rooted to the spot, terrified, as she waited for the next move. And Bithia too – what did she feel? Was there any conflict of loyalty as she looked at this tiny crying Jewish infant and thought of her father's plan for the elimination of his people?

All we do know is that Bithia faced the challenge with compassion. It didn't take her long to sum up the situation and make the decision to allow this Hebrew baby to live. The gentleness on her face as she peered at the infant must have given Miriam courage too. When she heard the princess suggest she would adopt the child, Miriam leapt eagerly forward and offered to find a Hebrew wet-nurse to feed him. There was nothing odd about this. Everyone would know that there were many Hebrew women whose babies had been wrenched from them, and whose milk had not dried up. Some of them would even be nursing children of Egyptian mothers whose milk might be inadequate. Bithia accepted the offer immediately, and Miriam ran to get her own mother.

Did the princess guess that Jochebed was the child's natural mother as she met her and offered to pay her for his support? As the three of them looked at each other in openness and trust, did Pharaoh's daughter suspect that Miriam was his sister? We have no idea. And it really didn't matter. Bithia's concern and compassion mirrored the love that shaped the actions of Jochebed and Miriam. For a short time, they were a trio of women together, united in the challenge of securing this baby's safety. They were women committed to securing life and not death for this one infant at least. And they succeeded.

So many interesting factors are wrapped together in the way these women met their challenge. Culture and politics certainly played a key part. They were thrown together over a particular political incident; one over which they had absolutely no say. The decision to eliminate Hebrew baby boys was imposed by the autocratic ruler, and they were simply three women outside the structures of influence. Yet the ramifications affected each one of them.

A second factor is related to power. The three women held very different levels of authority, yet each carefully exercised whatever power she had. Jochebed had the power of a mother's unconditional love for her newborn child. And that is powerful indeed. She responded with all the protection she could muster, to work out a plan, make a cradle and trust God. Miriam had the power of a nimble, quick-witted girl, who could use her own insignificance to advantage. She responded by watching over her brother without arousing suspicion, assessing Bithia's obvious compassion and then making her clever suggestion. Bithia had the power of a daughter of Pharaoh, with social and economic status and servants to do her bidding. She responded by using all these to adopt the baby, find childcare and ensure his survival. None of them had the power to change a barbaric, unjust law. Yet the joint weight of the power they did have meant that one baby escaped the consequences of that injustice to become a future leader anointed by God.

Facing our challenges today

The story offers us many insights into how, today, we might face challenges that seem beyond our control. The first is to be led by love and not fear. Jochebed and Miriam had much to lose if their actions were discovered, but they loved their baby more than they feared for themselves. When we are led by love rather than fear, we gain more courage, and God often empowers us to be stronger and to see things more clearly. The second is to assess what can be done with the power we hold. In this story an absolute ruler was imposing his will on oppressed people, but the women still found the power to resist. Today, at the most fundamental level we can all pray, resist injustice personally and raise issues in our churches. Even more, in these days of democracy and law, we can also hold leaders accountable, expose wrong-doing, address discrimination and stand up for those more vulnerable than ourselves. We probably have more power than we think.

The third insight we get is that working to face challenges together brings greater effectiveness. Jochebed could do something on her own, but far more with Miriam's companionship and help. Then with Bithia's intervention, the immediate problem was solved. Finding others of like mind, hearing the needs we share together and being committed to work with each other brings so many more possibilities within our grasp. We can even change laws by concerted action and advocacy.

Women of faith and love have been effecting change this way for centuries. Whether contesting slavery, the Mines and Factory Acts, promoting the need for education, votes for women or the rights of disabled people, concerted action is a powerful human tool for justice. Over the past year, Christian organizations like Restored, Beyond the Streets, Press Red and I-C Change have enabled women (and men) to come together and begin to make the world a more just place. We are still learning positively from Jochebed, Miriam and Bithia.

Questions to ponder

1 Can you think of any parallels through history when some women have had to protect their children from ruthless tyrannical regimes?
2 What initiatives do you know of in your area where women are involved in action to bring positive change?

3

The five daughters
of Zelophehad

NUMBERS 27.1–11

I wonder if these five names meant anything to you before you read the text: Mahlah, Noah, Hoglah, Milcah and Tirzah. I suspect not. The book of Numbers is a fairly unfamiliar part of the Bible. Yet the names of these five sisters who lived long ago have become a key part of the ancestral history of Jewish women. Because of the way the sisters handled a formidable challenge, a vital new chapter was created in the history of women in Israel.

The people of Israel had been wandering through the desert for 40 years since their escape from Egypt. They were now in the plains of Moab and in sight of the promised land. Moses was instructed by God to take a second census of the tribes of Israel. Most of the people listed in the first census 38 years ago in the desert were now dead, and Moses needed an up-to-date picture of the second generation. It was important to know how many men could serve in the army, and how to divide up the land that the people were about to enter. According to God's decree, the tribal locations were to be decided by drawing lots, and the promised land apportioned according to the 'number of names' in the census (Numbers 26). More land would be given to the larger tribes and less land to the smaller ones. The 23,000 Levites were counted separately because, as the priestly clan, they held no land but were given tithes and offerings from all the other tribes. So to find out which other tribes were larger and smaller the people needed to be counted again.

The ancestral names on the first census were, of course, all male. As we know, the early people of Israel were a patriarchal society. They assumed male leadership and authority and a woman's place was domestic and subordinate. The second census also counted only men, and it was expected that women would be included in the lineage of the males in their family. But thereby hung a problem for the five sisters. They were the daughters of Zelophehad, who had died, along with his generation, in the desert, and they had no brothers. They quickly realized they would find themselves without land or inheritance when they entered Canaan.

We might expect that women subject to patriarchal norms would react by simply accepting the decree and keeping silent. It would be normal for them to grumble about it among themselves, to roam into other women's tents to complain, but otherwise stay out of sight and work out how to make the best of it. They could probably marry and move into someone else's inheritance, raising children for another family line. Zelophehad's daughters, however, had different ideas. They came to a decision together and decided to make their case known. So, without being called by anyone, they went out of their tents – their female 'social space' – to the area where only the high-ranking men congregated, the sacred tent of meeting. This was where tablets from Sinai rested in the ark of the covenant, a place of great holiness and authority, and where women simply did not belong. Watching as these five women deliberately approached, some of the leaders present may have felt consternation, even alarm.

Standing before Moses, Eleazar the priest, the leaders, and indeed the whole community (Numbers 27.2), the sisters boldly appealed against the regulation. They had a clearly worked-out strategy. First, they presented their father's credentials. He had been a loyal Israelite, not part of the faction that had opposed God's will. He had died in the desert, not been killed in an insurrection, so clearly he was due some respect. Then, they mounted their case: their father's name and lineage should not be cut off from his clan just because he had no son. Finally, they made their appeal: 'Give us property among our father's relatives' (verse 4). The daughters themselves should be permitted to inherit his land portion in order to avoid this potential injustice to their father's name. Since their culture recognized a connection between landholding and preservation of a male name in family lineage, this was indeed a good argument to make.

This narrative tells us a good deal about these women. They knew their history, their culture and its traditions, and they knew their law. More than that, they recognized that, as it stood, the law was discriminatory: it did not take into account the unusual circumstances, in those days, of a man without sons. Yet the women were able to distinguish

17

between God's law, which they considered to be intrinsically fair, and human implementation, which was not. It was human agents not divine decree that they were questioning here. Consequently, they were ready to engage with their leaders and point out the unjust nature of the current situation. They had the skill to back up their case with persuasive arguments, but they still showed considerable trust in their leaders' readiness to listen.

Moses could have quickly dismissed them as out of order, and, moreover, resented the overt opposition to his ruling. It was, after all, as far as he was concerned, a decree given by God. He could have insisted that they leave the law to him and the elders and return to their prescribed roles as women. Religious leaders through the centuries have happily adopted this stance. However, he didn't. He reacted as a truly conscientious leader should act, questioning not the women's break of protocol but his own interpretation of the law. In tacitly admitting his own inability to assess the claims of the sisters without praying to God, he displayed both vulnerability and astute leadership. He took the matter back to God.

The outcome was breathtaking. God ruled in favour of the women: 'Zelophehad's daughters are right. You must give them property of their own among their father's relatives. Turn their father's property over to them.' Even more, God moved from this individual case to a new universal rule for the people of Israel: whenever a man died and had no sons, the daughters were to be given the inheritance, and a more equitable heritage was established for family lines in general. Later in the text, the safeguarding of Zelophehad's inheritance was woven into marriage laws too, and in a radical way. The daughters were free to choose their own marriage partner, but within the lineage of Zelophehad, so that the family heritage stayed intact (see Numbers 36).

Moses accepted and upheld God's ruling, again showing fine leadership. Yet we know from the rest of the history that he was not the one to carry it out. For he was part of the generation who died in the desert and did not enter the promised land. It fell to Joshua to ensure that God's ruling for the women came to pass. The story of the five sisters is picked up later in Joshua 17.3–6, where we read how it is completed. Moses' ruling is implemented and full justice is enacted: Mahlah, Noah, Hoglah, Milcah and Tirzah receive their inheritance in the land they have now entered. God's word had been heard, and God's promises delivered by God's people.

Facing our challenges today

We can reflect on so many issues embedded in this story. Singleness, boldness, justice and leadership are all part of the subtext. The sisters were unmarried, yet they refused to live with the stereotypes of women that had been passed down for generations of patriarchal living. Though they were single, they did not see their identity as dependent on getting married, and the new law effectively endorsed that. It affirmed them as valued members of their clan in their own right as single women. Even today, it is not unknown, even in some Christian circles, for some women to feel either subsumed under the identity of their husband or 'left out' if they are not partnered. Not so for these sisters. They knew their identity lay in their relationship with God and in God's understanding of their lives. And they were vindicated. For women in today's culture, it is crucially important to see our identity as women before God and not bound by human convention. For this is what releases us into the freedom to be who we are.

The boldness of these women rested on their level of knowledge and understanding as well as their character. Not least this included knowledge about God. They believed God to be a just God who could be relied upon to decree what was fair. Where culture parts company with divine will, culture should change. This encourages us too to get to know God better, through study, prayer and reading, especially the Gospels.

Justice-seeking is also dependent on understanding and boldness. We need to be able to discern between what is right and what is unjust, and have the wisdom to know how to respond. Knowing the affirmation of God on our own thinking and actions brings confidence to hold on to what is right. And we cannot contest injustice anywhere without boldness. Whistle-blowers are rarely popular, and people often close ranks against protestors. We might find ourselves the subject of scorn or disapproval, yet we might find too that we can make a difference. Like those five sisters we can bring change not just for one generation but for centuries to come.

We learn also about leadership. The women themselves showed leadership in recognizing injustice and taking their stand. Moses and the elders showed leadership in listening to the women and submitting their own opinions to God. Leadership is neither solitary nor gendered, neither authoritarian nor bombastic. It is shared, perceptive, open and often gentle. When the people of God exhibit this kind of leadership together, God's will can be done and God's kingdom come.

This story is rich in its lessons and encouragements for issues that face us today. And the story of these feisty women lives on in the lives of hundreds of others whose actions change structures for the better.

Questions to ponder

1 Why do you think the Israelites were left in the wilderness for so many years before they entered the 'promised land'?
2 What stands out for you as significant in Joshua 17.3–6 in the way the inheritance resolution was implemented for the five sisters?

4

Rahab: prostitute, traitor, role model

JOSHUA 2.1–24; 6.1–25

The story of Rahab would fit easily into any war narrative. Here was a courageous woman who defied the authorities and worked with spies. She put her own life on the line, and took formidable risks, which, if discovered, would have meant torture and death. Yet, unlike most traditional heroines, she was actually a traitor. She enabled the foreign agents to receive and pass on vital information which would bring her own people's downfall. And, to further complicate issues, she was a prostitute who sold sex for a living. So some might raise an eyebrow or two when they read the praise heaped on her by two New Testament writers. These authors mark her out as a forerunner of Christian faithfulness (James 2.25; Hebrews 11.31).

When the story in the book of Joshua opens, the Hebrews are encamped in the Jordan valley opposite Jericho. God has promised them that they will be led into a new land that is fertile and rich in natural resources, and where they will eventually live in peace and prosperity. But meanwhile, the land is occupied. And the king of Jericho is not disposed to giving up his territory to these incoming upstarts! So, if they are to reach their destination, it is important for Joshua to gain intelligence regarding the king's military strength. He sends out two spies.

The spies stayed in Rahab's house, which was built into the city wall. The house seems to have been multi-purpose, providing a family dwelling, an inn and a brothel. This was not uncommon in those days, and lodging in the inn did not entail buying sex. For the spies, this would have been an ideal location to gather intelligence. With people coming and going, wine flowing and soldiers visiting prostitutes, discretion often goes to the wind. Tongues are loosened. Quite quickly the spies can assess the forces they are up against. However, information goes in two directions, and messages get back to the king of Jericho that Israelite spies are in Rahab's house. This is not good news. The king sends his own envoys to Rahab and demands that she hand them over. We might well assume that the family would have been rewarded for complying with the reasonable requests of their ruler and eliminating danger for their people. Yet Rahab does not comply. Instead, she lies to the king.

The decision for Rahab must have been a difficult one. Most people are tribal in some way or other. Loyalty to the group or nation is one of the most common human characteristics. Most of us know where we belong and tend to defend our own people. So why did Rahab do the opposite? Why did she defy the king, switch sides and protect the spies? The story suggests two reasons.

The first reason is clearly fear. The reputation of the invading Israelites has gone well ahead of them. Rahab

23

and her neighbours have already heard of the parting of the Red Sea when the Israelites came out of Egypt, and the following destruction of the Amorites. As she graphically explains, 'our hearts melted in fear and everyone's courage failed because of you' (verse 11). But the second reason is much deeper. It is prophetic insight. She knows that God will give the Israelites the land. It is God's provision that they should have a dwelling place of their own, and nothing will ultimately prevent this. So she turns her back on her own Canaanite religion and acknowledges her belief that the God whom the Hebrews worship is the true God. It is a breathtaking statement of faith in the universality of God's rule: 'the LORD your God is God in heaven above and on the earth below.'

The soldiers sent to capture the spies have a wasted trip. They ask Rahab to bring out the Israelite men, but instead she has hidden them on the roof under bundles of flax. The barley harvest is the perfect time to dry flax and barley on the roof, and two human bodies cannot be distinguished in the bundles piled high. Then she constructs an elaborate story about the spies' departure and sends the soldiers off on a wild goose chase, carefully closing the gate after they are gone. Now the Israelite spies are safe and they can return to their camp. But before she lets them down the wall, she has business of her own to do.

Rahab is clearly a woman used to negotiation. She has lied to save the lives of two spies, effectively betraying her own people. The cost of this, if it were discovered, would certainly be death to her and her family. So now she asks for their lives to be spared when the Israelites enter the land. It is a perfectly reasonable request. The response from the spies is exactly what she hoped for: 'Our lives for your lives! . . . If you don't tell what we are doing, we will treat you kindly and faithfully when the LORD gives us the land' (verse 14). The promise is sealed with a physical sign, as so often in the culture of the people of Israel. A line of scarlet cord is given to her, which she is to place in the window through which the spies escape. When the Israelites enter the land, the spies themselves will make a priority of looking out for the scarlet cord. They will then go into the house to bring the whole family to safety.

We all know the story of the battle of Jericho. The noisy, seven days' march around the city and the subsequent collapse of the city walls has passed down history in all its graphic detail. Even today it is commemorated in song and film. Jericho becomes a place of carnage; everything in the city is destroyed. But the Israelite spies remain faithful to their word. Rahab's whole household is kept safe. Rahab herself is celebrated in Hebrew history as a Jewish convert, and some legends even suggest Joshua marries her, although no biblical text supports that. But the legacy is that her family and her descendants become part of the Israelite nation.

Interestingly, Rahab's story appears in two New Testament references: in the letter to the Hebrews and the book of James. In each, she is described as a prostitute. Yet the authors offer this label without judgement; it is simply a descriptive statement. It's also interesting that the passages commend her for two different reasons. The author of Hebrews celebrates her faith – alongside such key figures as

Moses, Joseph, Samuel and Gideon. The apostle James celebrates her works – noting that she did not simply believe but put her faith into practice. In both cases, she is offered to us as a role model from whose faith and actions we have much to learn.

Facing our challenges today

The story of Rahab speaks into our lives at different levels. First, it challenges our attitudes – for example, towards prostitution. We don't know why Rahab was a prostitute, but it was clearly related to the financial responsibilities to her family. With no husband on the scene, no older brother with resources, she seems to have been the one supporting her parents and younger siblings. So she runs an inn and sells her body. Everyone else depends on her. And this is the story of many women in prostitution across the world today.

Prostitution is a miserable way to bring money into the household. It opens women up to abuse, degradation, violence and even murder. On a global scale, most women enter prostitution through destitution, violation, drugs or coercion. Many are trafficked. The idea that they choose this as a way of life is rebuffed by thousands who have exited prostitution. Today, many Christian women have been led to work alongside prostitutes. In the UK, Beyond the Streets engages men and women in compassionate care for women who sell their bodies, linking with Christian safe houses, like Joanna House in Leeds. Their stories of women's lives paint a sad picture of what drives a woman in this direction. Internationally, the picture is much more linked with trafficking and violence. The International Christian Alliance on Prostitution (ICAP) does tireless work with some of the most vulnerable women in the world, helping to build them up to a place where they can finally exit this way of life. Rahab's story challenges us all to see beyond the prostitute to the woman, and respond to her with the love of Christ.

The story also challenges our attitudes to nationalism. Rahab was aware that God was judging her own people because they were caught up in idolatry. Perhaps we need to be more critically aware of what is wrong in our own nation and see beyond our own national borders. We can easily be myopic, elevating ourselves and judging others, without being ready to combat the corruption, racism, lies, profiteering and indifference on our own shores. We are not without serious defects in the Western world. Vulture funds, tax havens, weapons sales and land-grabbing from poorer countries have all been highlighted in the UK and USA in recent years, as well as internal racial attacks and child abuse. God surely challenges us to live more justly as responsible nations.

Most of all, we learn from Rahab's faith and action. Ultimately, she placed everything before the judgement of God and did what she could to serve God's purpose. In our busy lives today, with so many distractions and confusions, it is not easy to know clearly what God's purpose is for us. We need time to reflect, pray, read God's word and soak ourselves in the Gospels. And when we do, we might feel challenged to broaden our vision or change our minds, so we too become part of God's story for our future.

Questions to ponder

1 Why do you think the biblical passage sounds so non-judgemental about Rahab's prostitution?

2 What prevents us today from being more nationally self-critical as Christians?

5

Prophet, poet, judge: Deborah, leader of Israel

JUDGES 4 AND 5

We would be hard-pressed to find a woman of Deborah's credentials in our society today. She was a prophet, a poet, a leader of worship, a military strategist and, most of all, a judge. The judges in Israel provided leadership for the Israelites long before kings were anointed (beginning with Saul, around 1047 BC) and can be traced back to the time of Moses. He appointed specific people to seek God through prayer and meditation and then adjudicate in disputes. So people looked to Deborah to discern God's will and resolve disagreements justly.

We don't know many details about Deborah. Her name means 'bee' (or sometimes 'one who speaks'). From the text we might assume she had a husband called Lappidoth, but this interpretation is disputed by many Jewish scholars. They point out that 'Lappidoth' is a feminine plural noun, meaning 'torches', and couldn't really be a man's name. So 'wife of Lappidoth' might simply be referring to a place she came from. Because 'wife' and 'woman' are interchangeable in Hebrew, some scholars even translate the phrase as meaning 'a woman of fiery spirit'. Other scholars argue that if she had a husband, it was probably Barak, which puts an interesting spin on the story of the relationship between them. What is agreed by all, however, is that she was a leader of considerable authority, whose reputation for discerning divine guidance had spread across the tribes of Israel.

The place where Deborah held court is also interesting. It was 'under the Palm of Deborah between Ramah and Bethel in the hill country of Ephraim'. We hear a distant echo of the only other 'Deborah' in the Hebrew Scriptures. Wet-nurse to Rebekah mother of Jacob (later named Israel), she was buried beneath an oak tree to the south of Bethel. So a symbolic link exists between the Deborah who first nursed Israel and the Deborah who now held daily court as judge in Israel.

Judgement and prophecy went together in Deborah's calling. They were both badly needed. Many of the leading women of the Hebrew Scriptures lived during times of oppression and conflict, and this was true of Deborah. The Hebrews had entered Canaan about a century before and were living there as a loose confederation of tribes. They faced constant hostility from the Canaanites, especially from Jabin, the king of Canaan, and Sisera, the commander of his army. God's guidance for the way forward was badly needed.

When the story opens, Sisera has been oppressing the Israelites for 20 years. Deborah discerns it is time to challenge him. She summons Barak and instructs him to amass a huge force of Israelites to carry out God's purpose to bring an end to the cruelty and subjugation of their people. She prophesies God will lead Sisera and all his chariots and troops to the Kishon river where they will be defeated. However, in complete contrast to the decisiveness of Deborah, Barak shows reluctance, saying he won't take on this assignment unless she goes with him – a very strange response from a renowned military leader whose name means 'lightning'!

Is Barak rejecting Deborah's leadership here and challenging her prophetic judgement? It seems more likely that he is simply reacting from fear and insecurity. The Canaanites have a formidable army and Barak's troops stand no chance without God's intervention. Lacking self-confidence, he feels he needs Deborah to provide godly wisdom and discernment; unless she is with him, his mission will fail. Deborah's response is to chide and say that God will certainly defeat Sisera, but the glory will not go to Barak but to a woman. We assume that this woman will be Deborah, but we are in for a surprise.

The battle is as Deborah predicted. The huge force of Sisera's army and his nine thousand chariots is strangely routed, and defeated. Sisera escapes on foot and seeks refuge in the tent of someone he assumes to be an ally of King Jabin. It is a fatal mistake. After tending to his thirst and exhaustion, Jael, the wife of a blacksmith, allows him to fall into a deep sleep. Then she drives a tent peg through his skull, ending his reign of terror. Sisera has been brought down by a woman and Deborah's prophecies are fulfilled. King Jabin has lost his power, Israel is set free from his oppression, and peace will be maintained under the leadership of Deborah and Barak for 40 years. The victory song in Judges 5 gives all the glory to God for the rescue of his people.

The book of Judges recounts many stories of violence and terror. It makes uncomfortable reading for twenty-first-century readers. These were indeed bloodthirsty times, and both men and women were caught up in their horror. Only two women feature in this story, alongside thousands of male warriors, but together they produce a significant result for the people of Israel and usher in the longed-for peace. An interesting postscript to the story also exists. According to the Talmud, Sisera is the ancestor of one of the greatest figures in Jewish history, Rabbi Akiva. That a descendant of their great Canaanite enemy should become one of their own most renowned rabbinic scholars is surely a victory of peace for the Hebrew people. Deborah would have been delighted.

Deborah's whole ministry was one of facing challenges. Every day in holding court she would have needed God's wisdom and guidance to make sure justice was done. In discerning God's purpose for peace, she had to be sure she was hearing aright and not leading the people into folly and pointless bloodshed. In agreeing to accompany the men into battle, she needed the courage and commitment to see this through to the end. And in foreseeing how another woman would strike the final blow for peace she needed to leave the outcome to God.

Facing our challenges today

In our lives we often get glimpses of opportunities that God might be urging us to take where God might be leading, but we lack the commitment to make them happen. Deborah's story challenges us on this. She saw the whole thing through, even though it meant throwing her lot in with ten thousand warriors getting ready for battle! When the New Testament urges Christians to weigh up carefully what we are taking on, and to make sure we are prepared for the cost, we don't usually have anything quite this dramatic in mind! In our lives we are more likely to be held back by other circumstances like the pressure of events or just the tedious routines of life. We might feel we have a vision from God, where we experience a call to something new, yet never give the time to weigh up the possibility of taking this forward. It is all too easy to abandon the sense that we are being led in a new venture when the effort needed for making it work seems beyond us.

Those women who persist against all odds, and hold on to the vision that God has given them, can know amazing results of living in the centre of God's will. Even when it proves costly and demanding, the knowledge that this is their calling keeps them going. I think often of Lyn Lusi, who, along with her Congolese husband, set up Heal Africa, a Christian hospital in the midst of war-torn Goma, because she had heard the call of God. She faced exhaustion, emotional pain and relentless battles with authorities, as they cared for wounded civilians, rape victims and mutilated children. Yet that hospital has received constant protection and for decades it has been a beacon of hope and healing for so many broken and hurting people.

Deborah also teaches us about the importance of resisting things that are wrong. She knew that the way the Canaanites were oppressing the people of Israel was fundamentally unjust. It wasn't simply inconvenient, or something she didn't like. It was wrong. Many things that touch people's lives today are wrong, and unless we resist those things, and seek change, they will persist. Women outside the Church are often very good at this. They have set up women's refuges, helplines and aid centres for women subject to domestic violence or rape. They campaign for the release of political prisoners, unjustly incarcerated. They work for the protection of girls against grooming, and with prostitutes, helping them to exit. When Christian women join forces with these resisters, bridges are built to the faith, and the outworking of the gospel becomes more evident.

Finally, Deborah is confident about her role as a woman and upholds her calling before God. She does not bow to the authority even of Barak, but knows she is being asked to direct and guide him. Today, Christian women in every culture can be similarly confident that God is calling them to take leadership in all walks of life. There is no 'sacred–secular' divide; we need the empowering of the Holy Spirit in whatever area God leads. And leadership is not always in public office or official role. Sometimes it is quiet and unassuming, perceptively steering from the back, offering insights to others. Real leaders are women of prayer and discernment. For we all need to walk humbly, love mercy and act justly, knowing that the motivation can never be self-aggrandisement or praise from others, but simply service of God.

Questions to ponder

1 What difficulties do you have in reading the book of Judges? What, in your own reading, do you see as the overall messages of the book?

2 Are there any aspects of Deborah's leadership that you think women should try to emulate today? Are there aspects you would want to reject?

6

A tale of three widows

RUTH 1.1–22

The death of a husband brings both loss and upheaval in a woman's life. But when she lives in a foreign country, far from her own family, that loss can be magnified. And when a few years later she loses both her sons also, we can imagine she would be utterly inconsolable and the sense of abandonment would be enormous. That is Naomi's experience at the beginning of the book of Ruth.

Naomi lived with her husband Elimelech in Bethlehem in Judah at the time of the Judges. Jewish tradition suggests that Elimelech was a wealthy leader of considerable stature, with responsibilities in the community. But when a famine afflicts Israel he can no longer face the pressure from people around him to provide for them all. So he takes his wife and two sons away to visit Moab. Even though the Moabites have a different culture and worship different gods, Elimelech decides they will remain there. It is a tragic decision.

Naomi becomes a widow in Moab, for Elimelech dies. Then her sons marry. This is probably after their father's death as he would not have approved of them taking non-Jewish brides, and their wives are Moabites. Tradition suggests that Orpah and Ruth may have been sisters, possibly related to Moab's royal dynasty. They are happy marriages. Naomi grows close to her daughters-in-law, but no children are born. Then, tragedy strikes a second time. Naomi's two sons die. No explanation is given for their early deaths; we are simply left to guess. What we do know is that all three of the women are now widows, and they face a very uncertain future.

The urgent question for them all is what to do now. The challenges of widowhood are acute. To have no family support in a patriarchal society is likely to bring hardship and even destitution. The women can face this new challenge together but each one will need to make her own decision in the light of circumstances. Both younger women have the option of going home to their families; no doubt they would be received with welcome and given comfort. But what about Naomi? How can an older, isolated, Jewish widow cope with the loss of all her male providers, in a foreign land?

The news that the famine has ended in Israel brings an immediate possibility. Naomi can return home. Surely her male relatives in Bethlehem would take pity on her and provide support. She will not be destitute. At the very least, she can depend on the Jewish tradition of gleaning, where she will be free to go over the farmers' fields after harvest, to pick the grain or crops left for the poor. This solution seems good. So preparations begin and her daughters-in-law resolve to go with her. They both love Naomi. They loved her sons. They have already shared both joy and intense grief with each other. What's more, they know something of the Jewish faith. A new life in Judah seems to make sense for them all. Arrangements completed, they gather everything they need for the journey and set out for the road ahead.

They have not travelled far, however, before Naomi has a strong pang of conscience. How can she take Orpah and Ruth away from their own country? They are still young and could have children, but what chance would Moabite women have of finding husbands in Judah? She halts the travel, and we can imagine the distress and tears as Naomi tells them there is nothing she can offer them in Israel. Each of them belongs in Moab and should go back to their own mother. Three times she urges them to stay behind and twice they both resist. Eventually, the final decision is made. Orpah chooses to remain in Moab, and Ruth chooses to go with Naomi. In actions pregnant with symbolic significance, Orpah weeps and kisses Naomi goodbye, and Ruth weeps but cleaves firmly to her.

We see the extent of Ruth's commitment to Naomi in her eloquent, emotional outburst. It contains one of the most powerful and moving statements found anywhere in the Hebrew Scriptures: 'Where you go I will go, and where you stay I will stay. Your people will be my people and your God my God. Where you die I will die, and there I will be buried.' Her attachment to Naomi is so great that Ruth promises before God that even death will not separate them.

We can glimpse something of the heart of each woman in those decisions they took. Naomi loved the young women, and wanted the best for her daughters-in-law, even if it reinforced her own loneliness. Orpah loved Naomi, but was ultimately unsure about leaving the life she had known in Moab and risking the unknown, and so she drew back.

But Ruth was ready to trust not just Naomi but Naomi's God. Ruth was willing to let go of her Moabite past, separate herself from her own kinsfolk and pledge complete faithfulness to her mother-in-law. For the rest of her days she would be Naomi's daughter and would worship God. The bond between the two women had become both emotional and spiritual, and would become even stronger as they faced their lives ahead.

Once Orpah turns back, we hear nothing more of her. The Jewish Talmud suggests she returned to her country's idols, lived promiscuously, and eventually married into a family of giants. The rabbis identify her with Rapha (or Harafah), the mother of Goliath and of the four warriors of Gath, who appear in 2 Samuel 21. They see the parting of the sisters-in-law spiritually echoed in the mortal combat between David and Goliath in 1 Samuel 17. Whatever the history, it is very likely that the choice Orpah made was, sadly, not one that brought her closer to God.

We do know what happens to Naomi and Ruth, however, for the rest of the book of Ruth follows it through. With contacts and advice from her mother-in-law, Ruth marries Naomi's kinsman, Boaz, and they have children. Their great grandson will be David, who fights Goliath and will be king of Israel. David leaves his legacy too as author of many of the psalms. Naomi and Ruth's response to the challenge of their widowhood releases God's power to their nation. Through them, all Israel is blessed. Even more than that, in centuries to come, through Ruth and David's line a special birth will take place. The child's name will be Jesus, and he will be the Saviour of the world.

Facing our challenges today

The challenge of commitment is so demanding, for it stretches out into the future. Today we live in an era where such commitment has become counter-cultural. Commitment to church, to community, to friendship, even to family does not lie easily in societies with ingrained individualism, where we are invited to put ourselves first all the time. People are increasingly consumers rather than committers, urged always to try out new things, new leisure pursuits, new partners, even new churches, to see whether they suit them. Being committed for the long haul to a venture, a group of people, or to supporting those who need us, may present struggles we would rather avoid. But it may also be part of our calling as Christians.

The challenge of taking risks leaps out of this passage. The three women were forced out of their comfort zone with the deaths of their husbands and sons. But the risks for each were different. For Naomi, they were related to growing old and facing the demands of an arduous journey. For Orpah and Ruth, they were related to leaving everything behind and going to a place they knew little about. In our own lives there are times when we are challenged to take risks without having any idea of what might lie ahead. Moving home, giving up work, church planting, adopting children, taking on service overseas are all aspects of God's calling to us. And facing the choice of staying as we are or moving on and stepping out into the unknown can be a difficult experience. Yet we never do this relying on our own strength or ideas. When we know this is God's call, we know also we can rely on God never to abandon us, but to see us through.

One other important challenge comes out in this story – that of keeping on. After her declaration to Naomi, Ruth never looked back. Jesus reminds us in the Gospels not to put our hand to the plough and then turn back. St Paul describes how he let go of what lay behind, fixed his vision ahead and pressed on in faith towards the goal. We need these reminders. Our human temptation is often to look over our shoulder at what might have been, to long to go back and take a different route. Sometimes, of course, we might have to retrace our steps if we find we are at a dead end. Sometimes we find we are in a fallow season, or that the way has suddenly got harder. But still we are called to keep on and walk by faith rather than by sight.

When we step out in trust, we often discover that God is always calling us forward, always leading us on. And through prayer we can find hope and perseverance for the way ahead. Keeping on has been the testimony of faithful Christians through the ages. So many of them, even in the most unexpected parts of the journey, when they have given their lives fully into God's care and God's service, have found the strength they need to see the journey through.

Questions to ponder

1 How do you think Naomi's faith stayed steadfast in a country that practised idolatry?
2 Widowhood was very difficult in early societies. In what areas in our own culture do widows struggle today?

7

Hannah: not drinking but praying

1 SAMUEL 1—2

The longing to be a mother is an emotion known to millions of women down through the ages. The ordeal of seeing their friends become totally absorbed in mother-hood and babies can be overwhelming for those who are childless. Singleness or infertility does not take away the longing to be a mother, and the experience of empty arms when so many others have little ones to cuddle can be painful indeed. In some cultures childlessness is a massive social barrier too, because having children is the key role of a woman there. So in addition to the constant pain of un-fulfilled longings, women who have never given birth can face pity or ostracism from women who have.

People in ancient Israel believed that a large family was a blessing from God: they even sang songs about it (Psalm 127). The downside of such respect for maternity was that infertility was a source of shame. The wives of the early patriarchs, Sarah, Rebekah and Rachel, had all endured the misery of not being able to conceive (Genesis 18, 25, 30) and had not handled it well. In Hannah's story, in the first book of Samuel, she faced the same situation. Despite having a kind and loving husband, who treasured her for who she was, she longed for a child to love. To make matters worse, this was a polygamous culture, and her husband Elkanah's other wife, Peninnah, had no problems at all in conceiving. The relationship between the two women was not good. Peninnah suspected that Hannah was really the favoured wife of their husband, and compensated for this by scorning and humiliating her rival.

Each year the family took the pilgrimage to Shiloh, to worship God, and each year the taunting got worse. Peninnah flung her barbs until Hannah wept and couldn't eat. Even the ritual process of distributing portions of meat to wives and children reinforced Hannah's misery. Wanting to convince Hannah of his love and respect, her husband gave her a double portion of food, but all that did was to remind Hannah that she had no children to share it with. One year she could bear Peninnah's stinging insults no more. Consumed with grief, she left the gathering in tears and went off to pray. She was unaware, however, that she was being watched by Eli, the temple priest. Eli was not impressed by the state Hannah was in. He thought she was drunk. It was an easy conclusion to draw; a lot of wine was flowing, and Hannah was thrashing around, displaying unguarded emotions. She would know that Hebrew prayers were normally said out loud, but no words were coming from her mouth. It is easy to see why Hannah's moving lips seemed to Eli a sign of intoxication rather than silent prayer. He rebuked her for her impropriety.

He was able to change his mind quickly, however. This misinterpretation and reprimand brought an immediate, tearful response from Hannah. No, she was not drunk. Far from it! She was praying to God in sheer desperation. The old priest was a compassionate man and quickly understood. His judgement had been wrong. Without knowing the content of her prayer, he warmly joined in and asked that God might grant her plea. This empathy and blessing must have been a real source of peace to Hannah. It must also have given her increased hope. Eli was not to know that Hannah was asking God that she should bear a son. Even less was he to know that God's answer would deeply affect his own life. Hannah's promise, that she would give back to God a son born to her, would involve Eli. He would be given the responsibility of teaching God's way to this boy, and show him how to serve in the temple. Unknown to himself, Eli was praying a prayer that would involve him in preparing a key servant of God for lifelong service.

The discovery that she was pregnant must have made Hannah excited and ecstatic. The birth of their son Samuel completed her joy. But the next months that passed brought a different challenge for her. The challenge of childlessness was now replaced by the challenge of fulfilling her promise to God. Samuel's time in the family would be temporary. After the first two euphoric years, every day must have been a quiet step closer to another kind of grief – that of separation and loss. Each anniversary of the prayer in the temple was a reminder that they must return. Did Hannah regret that promise made in her moment of desperation? The story suggests that this never crossed her mind. Although she knew that Samuel would not be with her throughout his childhood, Hannah did not shy away from the commitment she had made on that emotional night. A promise to God is a matter of covenant. God had been faithful to her; now it was her turn to respond. Encouraged by Elkanah, whose loss of his young son would also be great, she was fully resolved to honour her pledge.

So Samuel stayed at home with Hannah until after he was 'weaned', which, in those days, would probably have been around the age of five. During those years there was much preparation to do for his life ahead. Hannah would have begun her son's education. She and Elkanah would have passed on their faith in God and taught him more about God. They would have tried, gently and lovingly, to prepare him for the changes he would experience when he left their home. And the time eventually came. Probably during the annual pilgrimage, sometime after Samuel's sixth birthday, the family returned to Shiloh to sacrifice and worship. Eli would be there guiding the pilgrims. The moment had come to draw him back into the story of Hannah's prayer, Samuel's birth and Hannah's promise.

Whatever preparations Hannah had gone through, however, Eli had not! We can imagine the old priest's face when Hannah came to him and reminded him of their encounter all those years before. He now heard, with awe, what had been the prayer of her heart. Even more, he was given the news that she was about to place God's answer to her prayer, her precious son, into his care. It must have been a moment of utter shock for Eli. But it can only have been followed by praise and thankfulness to God. We find later in the story that Eli's own sons cared little about God or their father's faithfulness to his service. But now, this little son of Hannah was to take their place. Despite his young age, he would shoulder new responsibilities with spiritual maturity. We have little idea of what went through the young boy's mind as he said his goodbyes. His parents would return each year, but for a child so young this wait must have felt like an eternity. For his mother too, the loss would have brought desolation. Yet as Samuel stayed with Eli, the old man's prayers that Hannah would bear more children were answered, and her days of childlessness were over for ever.

Hannah's strong character is shown throughout the story. She needed it to face the challenge of domestic friction. It takes a lot to cope with taunts from another woman, especially when that woman is your husband's other wife! The grief over her childlessness made Hannah very vulnerable. Peninnah's sneering clearly found its target and wounded her. Yet there is no indication that Hannah resorted to insults in return, or even tried to turn Elkanah against her rival. She absorbed the hurt and took her pain to God.

Prayer features significantly in the story. Prayer, for Hannah, was not limited to the formal words prescribed in the temple, for she also felt free to speak to God from the depths of her heart. She could do this, however deep her pain and her humiliation before others, because she believed that God cared. She was coming to a personal deity not an abstract force, and she trusted God and felt she would be understood.

Faithfulness also is highlighted; the cost of faithfulness is the biggest challenge in the story. For it meant letting go of someone she loved so much. It meant parting with her little son and trusting him to a man he didn't know. Yet Hannah's word was important. What she had promised she would fulfil, whatever the sacrifice. We can only guess what emotional loss Hannah experienced in committing her son to God's service and returning home without her child. Only the knowledge that she had been faithful to God could have got her through those first months after the return from Shiloh. Yet her faithfulness was to have an impact on the lives of her people in ways she could never have imagined.

Facing our challenges today

Many people today might find aspects of Hannah's decision very strange. There are few contemporary parallels in the West to leaving a small son behind with an older man to serve in the temple. Modern UK safeguarding might question whether this was appropriate for a six-year-old. Yet there are similarities in many cultures. I have met elderly men across the world who are currently bringing up small children, as the generation in between has died of AIDS. And it was only a century or so ago in English culture when many children of public figures would leave home to go away to school at the age of seven. It was not unusual for them to spend the next ten years preparing for public service in the colonies and go overseas in their teens.

Hannah's longings, however, are familiar still today. The challenge of childlessness does not get any easier, however advanced the society in which we live. Even with artificial insemination, adoption and surrogacy, many women still have to live with an unfulfilled desire to have a child. Hannah's story encourages us to bring our longings to God. I know women who have prayed about infertility – indeed, I have prayed with them myself – and seen the answer to their prayers in the faces of lovely children.

However, praying is probably the easiest challenge to meet. A much harder challenge is to go on believing when prayers are not answered and longings are not met. That's why some women find the story of Hannah painful to read. Their biological clocks are ticking away, and they have never been pregnant. Others have struggled with miscarriage; yet others experience a roller coaster of emotions as, repeatedly, they find themselves unable to bring a pregnancy to full term. Yet Hannah's story urges them not to pretend there's no pain in all this. Denial of the hurt we go through can lead to resentment towards those with children, and hardness of heart against God.

We can be honest with God about heartache, for God already knows how we feel. Like the psalmist, we have God's permission to weep or to rebuke God for unanswered prayer. Lament can help us to find resources to live more effectively with disappointment and to see a bigger picture of God's will for our lives.

For many women, serving God does not mean nurturing and bringing up their own children. It might mean giving our time to serve God in spontaneous and unexpected ways, responding to needs all around us, of others who crave our nurture. It might be to develop the emotional resources to reach out to those who have been badly parented, or had their young hearts broken; to adopt youngsters whose experience of being parented is fragmented, to volunteer in safe houses for street girls, or refuges for the abused. Ours is a society where brokenness, isolation, neglect and anger eat people alive, and it desperately needs Christians to provide the love and understanding that brings people hope.

God gave Hannah the son she longed for, but then took him from her for his service. Hannah's new loneliness without him may well have been greater than any she had experienced before. The challenge of faithfulness can make us feel alone, leading us into places we would rather not go. Yet when God gives us the gift of feeling, we can enter empathetically into the pain of others. And so many have found that when they share what it means to struggle with loss, bereavement, disability or unfulfilled hopes, they realize that their own loneliness is swallowed up in service.

Questions to ponder

1 How would you rank the list of things that made Hannah unhappy before Samuel was born? What do you think was the worst of them?
2 What breakthroughs in prayer have you known in your life? How do you cope with prayer that seems to be unanswered?

8

Abigail saves the day

1 SAMUEL 25.2–19

I wonder if you've ever been surprised to find that one of your beautiful intelligent friends has married a disagreeable, ignorant, boorish man. You suddenly find that visiting her is no longer a pleasure but an embarrassment. You never know what to make of the attitudes he displays or the inappropriate comments he makes; you find him simply unpleasant. In the book of Samuel, Abigail's husband fits that description very accurately. And it leaves Abigail in some very difficult situations. One of them almost reaches crisis point.

Abigail's story is set in the conflict between King Saul and Israel's hero, David. Samuel, now a prophet, first anoints Saul as king of Israel and then David as his eventual successor. After David defeats Goliath, the great champion of the Philistines, he is showered with admiration, and the people celebrate him. Meanwhile, King Saul's popularity spirals into decline and he himself becomes bitter and resentful. Losing the integrity he once had, Saul allows his jealousy of David to become all-consuming, and even tries to kill him.

When our story opens, David has become a fugitive, knowing that his life is in danger from King Saul. It is unsafe to stay in one place for too long, so David and his men move around into parts of the country rich enough to support them. A vast wilderness area, Paran lies west of the southern end of the Dead Sea. Though the land is not very fertile, it is good for raising sheep and goats. Here we find Abigail and her husband Nabal, who raises substantial flocks that bring him wealth. It is in this area too that David and his men now go to seek refuge.

Nabal and Abigail's marriage was almost certainly arranged by their families; it seems unlikely that Abigail, given a choice, would ever have chosen Nabal for a husband! But, on the whole, women were not given a choice. Nabal's name means 'fool', and the Bible's description of him as 'surly and mean' conveys the absence of anything pleasant or attractive in his character. By contrast, Abigail is described as engaging, intelligent and beautiful, and her name means 'father's joy'. It is difficult to imagine a couple of greater contrast. What's more, there seems little doubt about which one of the couple is more respected. Nevertheless, they live together with their extended household in Maon, and Nabal's wealth brings them a comfortable life.

The incidents in the narrative occurred during the shearing period, which was a very festive season of great hospitality. David and his men sought refuge in the area and acted with responsibility and care towards Nabal's flocks. Unlike many fugitives, they showed respect for his ownership; they hadn't taken any of the sheep or goats for their own food, but in fact protected both them and the shepherds against predators: animal and human. Then came festival time; it was a time for David and his group to enjoy neighbourly hospitality.

Knowing that Nabal was in the area, David sent his men to greet him and request provisions.

The approach of the men, on behalf of David, was undertaken with all the customary formal courtesy. They wished blessings, health and long life for him and his household. As credentials of their own good faith, they explained how they had offered protection to Nabal's flocks. Now, if Nabal might donate some provisions (always the case during festivals), David would like to receive them and share the festivities. This perfectly normal request recognized the Jewish responsibility for sharing abundance and offering hospitality to those in need. It was an honour to receive guests, and an entreaty from a hero like David would normally have been met with great generosity. In itself, it called for a celebration.

Unfortunately, Nabal was not into courtesy or tradition. His response was churlish, offensive and nasty. His immediate dismissal, 'Who is this David?' could not have been construed as anything but an insult. Everyone knew who David was and sang his praises (1 Samuel 18.7). They also knew the problems David faced because of Saul, and most people would have been only too glad to help him. Nabal, however, wasn't one of them. He completely dismissed the kind service David's men had voluntarily provided for his flock and ignored their predicament. Interested only in himself, he rudely indicated he had no intention of taking provisions from his shearers to give to David. It was an appallingly foolish reaction. With scorn and abuse ringing in their ears, David's men returned to their leader.

Unsurprisingly, David took the insult personally. Who

wouldn't? Furious, and with four hundred armed men, he set off to confront Nabal in the middle of festivities. At this point in the story, Abigail was drawn in. When one of the servants went to her and described the interaction, her heart must have sunk. Nabal's rude rebuff to the courteous greeting of David's men would have sounded all too familiar. David's men had gone the extra mile for Nabal's shepherds – effectively becoming a wall shielding them day and night. And all they got in return were Nabal's crass insults. The lack of courtesy and hospitality would have turned Abigail cold. She would also have seen immediately that, because of Nabal's boorishness, the whole household faced a very dangerous predicament.

It is interesting that the servant ran to Nabal's wife with his fears and not his master. It was probably because stubborn, egoistic and churlish men don't readily listen and change their minds! The man probably agreed with the biblical description of him as 'a wicked fool' and preferred Abigail's wisdom and discretion. It suggests too that this may not have been the first time she was drawn in to bypass her husband and save the day.

Abigail listened readily and understood the issue was urgent. A large trained army, ready for battle, was effectively marching on them. What's more, whatever action she took had to be behind her husband's back. Fool that he was, he would have stopped her and brought disaster on them all. The story writer is keen for us to know every detail of the sumptuous provisions Abigail now got ready: 5 ready-dressed sheep, 500 measures of corn, 200 loaves, 2 huge skins of wine, 100 cakes of raisins and 200 pressed figs! We can imagine her relief as the servants led donkeys carrying the bounty ahead of her.

It must have been some encounter when Abigail, the servants and the laden donkeys halted in front of David's army. Facing 400 armed men bent on wiping out Nabal's folk, Abigail had planned her strategy carefully. As soon as she saw David, she dismounted and threw herself to the ground in respect. The wisdom of her humility, as she greeted David, was in marked contrast to the folly of Nabal's arrogance. Begging David to ignore her stupid husband, and offering herself as the one to blame, was a well-planned move. Now she could offer to make up for her lack of awareness and bring all the provisions David and his men could need.

Abigail went further than offering provisions, however. She poured prophetic blessings on David, praying that his life and safety would always be in the protective care of God. She prayed that he would be kept free from all wrongdoing, and that the 'staggering burden of needless bloodshed' would not be on his hands. These were not the words of a woman in subjection, but of a wise prophet and confident leader of Israel. She had worked out immediately what was wrong, knew what would put it right and took immediate action. All the qualities of wisdom and leadership were demonstrated by Abigail and she assumed that her mission would be successful. Nabal might show no remorse, yet she would act without his knowledge or consent and offer repentance on his behalf. This way she could ensure reconciliation and safety for her household.

David's response was as she hoped and expected. He

praised God for sending Abigail, blessed her for having kept him from shedding blood, accepted her gifts and food, and sent her home in peace. Relief and rejoicing must have been evident from the servants who witnessed the whole drama. Back home, unaware of the danger he had put them in, or that his wife had saved the day, Nabal was throwing a king's feast and getting very drunk. When he heard Abigail's confession the next morning, he suffered a heart attack. Within a week he was dead.

Surprised but clearly delighted at this unexpected outcome, David wasted no time in asking Abigail to be his wife. Her wisdom would be steering many of his better policies as king. So Abigail became a second wife to David and they had one son, Chileab. Beyond that, we know nothing more of her. We don't know whether she was still alive when David became enamoured with Bathsheba and made her pregnant; we don't know if she heard the rebukes of Nathan to David, after he ruthlessly brought about the death of Bathsheba's husband (2 Samuel 11.2–5; 12.1–14). We don't know how well she got on with the other women in David's harem. But we do know that many of the restrictions she faced as Nabal's wife would have continued in David's household. For the structures of patriarchy were still alive and well, and would have continued to have an impact on Abigail's life.

Facing our challenges today

Abigail's story offers us so many insights for coping with impossible situations. She models how we can react when relationships have got out of hand. First, she is approach-able. Second, she thinks fast, allowing her own instinct and knowledge to direct her as to where the danger is. Third, she comes up with a reconciliation plan – equating to what her husband *should* have done. Fourth, she enlists the help of those she can trust, and, finally, she carries it out. Abigail puts peace at the top of her desired outcomes – more than preserving her own security or placating her husband.

We often find it hard to think and act quickly. Yet most of us know that putting off an urgent problem usually makes it worse, especially where this involves conflict with another person. Rather than running from the problem, harbouring resentment or feeling self-righteous, seeking out that person is wise counsel. It makes enormous sense to clear away misunderstandings swiftly and offer apologies where appropriate. The generosity we show in resolving conflict could well affect the future course of our own lives. Relationships that are not healed fester, and the wounds can become permanent.

Abigail also teaches us about discretion. Sometimes we have to quietly follow our own intuition to bring about right outcomes, even when it means stepping out of line, especially in a context where women have little authority and no power. But even in our culture discreet conciliatory action is often more helpful at work or in family life than arguing with others about what should be done. Of course, sooner or later we will need to make public what we have done. But when decisions are wise, other people eventually welcome them, and hopefully don't suffer heart attacks.

Women throughout the ages have been good at

peacemaking. Often this has been on a public stage. Women have been at the forefront of peace advocacy in the UK, from the Women's International Movement for Peace (founded in 1915 and active throughout the twentieth century) to the Greenham Common Peace Camps in the 1980s and women's peace activity in Northern Ireland. On a global scale, women have formed coalitions to urge those in conflict into negotiation and peace talks rather than bomb each other out of existence. Christian women follow Jesus, the Prince of Peace, so it is a very clear calling and reflected in many Christian pacifist groups across the world.

Today, wise women are vitally needed. When international male leaders and rulers exhibit folly not unlike Nabal's, we urgently need contemporary Abigails to sound a different note. It only needs a few individuals to take the first initiative, encouraging strategies that work against the escalation of conflict and for the reconciliation of nations. From simple beginnings tipping points for peace can be reached. We can change the course of history when we convince people that peaceful and generous co-existence will always be better than war.

Questions to ponder

1 Why do you think Nabal was so inept at courteous relationships? Do you think churches could help awkward people to develop better 'people skills'?
2 Can you give reasons why women were predominant in peace movements throughout the twentieth century?

9

The wise woman of Abel Beth Maakah

2 SAMUEL 20

Abel Beth Maakah is not a place name that is commonly found in twenty-first-century tourist brochures. However, in the time of the prophet Samuel, it was a significant location, a substantial fortified city in northern Israel. People could run into the city as a place of safety and refuge. David was now king, and Saul was long gone, but it was not a time of peace. With continual hostilities during King David's reign between the 'people of Judah' (David's tribe of origin in the south) and the 'people of Israel' (the ten northern tribes), such places of safety were very necessary.

When this story opens, the political and military tensions were at their height. There had been an attempted insurrection, led by Absalom, King David's son. Other members of David's family were also involved; some nephews backed Absalom, and others stayed loyal to the king. One of the nephews most faithful to King David was Joab, a renowned military leader. He pursued the opposing army and killed Absalom, ending his insurrection (2 Samuel 19.41–43). With David's rebellious son out of the way, surely there could now be a time of peace?

Joab, however, got no gratitude from David. Instead, the king was devastated. His kingdom might have been saved but his son was dead. What was more, this was in direct disobedience to his own command that Absalom's life was to be spared. In his anger and grief he rounded on his faithful general and took Joab's command away. Another nephew, Amasa, was the one who was put in charge. This was a very bad move. As one of Absalom's henchmen, Amasa was not to be trusted. Amasa was killed by Joab, but not before he had colluded with a Benjaminite, Sheba, to mount a new insurrection. So now Sheba carried on the opposition against David.

Sheba, however, grossly underestimated what he was up against. He had called for help from the northern tribes but he was no match for David's army. And Joab was in charge again. With the army closing in on him, it was time for Sheba to find a safe refuge. So he ran into the city of Abel Beth Maakah. Surrounded by two enormous walls, the city must have seemed impregnable, and he himself was confident he would remain safe.

The city was strong but not impregnable. And now other people, not simply Sheba, were inevitably caught up in this skirmish. This safe refuge was set to become a site of battle. Joab had weapons and troops that could batter its ramparts, destroy its fortifications and bring the whole city to its knees. Effectively besieged inside the walls, every single inhabitant was in danger of being wiped out. As Joab's army began building ramps and systematically constructing their way in, it looked as if this would be the most likely outcome. In almost no time, the soldiers were able to scale the outer wall and begin the heavy battering of the inner wall. The lives of all the families in Abel Beth Maakah were in peril.

Then something quite extraordinary happened. A woman shouted across the ramps and asked that Joab speak to her. The assaulting army stopped. Why? It does seem amazing that Joab should hold up his military mission of vengeance and annihilation at the request of a woman. Yet he did. Joab indicated that he was ready to listen. This was also astonishing. Joab was a fierce, righteous warrior, doing whatever was necessary to defend the rule of King David. No man had ever tried to negotiate with him, and he certainly wasn't used to someone calling him out to stop! Yet he was also a careful military leader who weighed things up and made his own decisions. His decision now was to hear her out. So who was this woman, and how did she elicit such a response?

The name of the shouting woman is not disclosed in the story. She is simply called the 'wise woman'. She was probably a judge, or at least an accepted civic leader, and this fact would have been communicated to Joab. The fact that he stopped to listen to her indicates that, even in the patriarchal cultures of Israel and Judah, some women did command considerable authority. This woman clearly had influence, and not only among her own northern people but even outside the city walls. The rest of the city accepted her influence. No one questioned her leadership in opening the encounter with Joab. When we read her shrewd words to the invading commander, we begin to realize why.

The wise woman's strategy was a prudent one. It was not to plead or cajole but simply to call for justice and peace. She identified herself as one of the 'peaceable and faithful in Israel' (20.19). She identified her city as one where wisdom had long been cherished, for it was a 'mother in Israel'. The people in the city were God-fearing. They were faithful to God's divine rule. So why on earth was Joab about to slaughter them? As her speech reached a climax, she accused Joab of seeking to destroy the Lord's inheritance.

Her words hit their target. Joab's response was to back off immediately. 'Far be it from me that I should swallow up or destroy!' Instead, he decided to offer a compromise. They simply wanted the man who was leading the insurrection against the king. If Sheba were handed over to Joab, he and his troops would withdraw and leave them all in peace. The city would not be punished for harbouring a traitor.

The wise woman agreed to his demand, and her authority was accepted. Yet she made some modifications. The people did not hand Sheba over alive. If they had done that, who knows what prolonged torture or brutality the troops might have inflicted on him before Joab ordered his execution? After all, the wise woman had said she was 'peaceable in Israel'. Peace was being offered to the city, though it was on Joab's terms. So she changed the terms. The local elders made their own judgement on Sheba, convicted him, and then swiftly served his death sentence themselves. That done, they returned his severed head over the wall to Joab as evidence that the execution had been carried out. His death was a compromise for peace, yet under their jurisdiction it could be a more just undertaking. Alive or dead, the army had got its traitor, so the troops left and the city was saved.

The story gives us many insights into the political and military upheaval in biblical times. When we put this woman's actions against the backcloth of the harsh brutality of a fighting force, her courage and initiative become all the more remarkable. Yet, underneath the brutal fighting and killing, the people of Israel and Judah recognized the Torah as God's law, with all its moral teachings. This woman was reminding the military leader that both they and he stood under the judgement of God. He recognized the truth of her words, accepted them and responded.

An interesting link with the New Testament shows that this woman was not only a wise and brave mediator but also a prophet. By reinforcing the maxim that it is better for one person to die rather than that the whole people should perish, she was anticipating a statement that would be made many centuries later. In the Gospel of John, the high priest Caiaphas cited exactly that point before Jesus' crucifixion. So this woman's decision over Sheba connects us unexpectedly with the death of Jesus. In both cases, one person dies and the people are saved. The difference, however, remains fundamental. Sheba died for the sins he had committed. Jesus died for the sins we have committed.

Facing our challenges today

In many countries today, where religion and military power are bound up together, an intervention like this could well end up with the woman's death. Through the centuries, women have been victimized in such contexts. We have so many examples of brave women journalists, lawyers or even doctors who have been murdered for daring to criticize the power of their leaders. Few despots today acknowledge God's authority over them. It was that authority that lay behind this woman's wisdom and knowledge, and gave her confidence.

This woman spoke nonetheless, and the future of the city depended on her words. She did not mind standing out as a woman in a very male environment. There is nothing woman-affirming in a situation where walls are being battered down and people face destruction. Similarly, I have met brave Christian women in the Congo and elsewhere who have rebuked military leaders for violating the defenceless or allowing rape, and who have called for justice. And their actions and advocacy have brought changes in the law. Today we need those who stand against military might to ensure protection for the vulnerable, restraint in conflict, and to move cultures towards greater justice.

Women today who are to be leaders in the public arena or in the Church are most effective when they speak from a background of learning and understanding. Speaking from a position of ignorance isn't spiritual and it can be dangerous. Without wisdom grounded in knowledge, leaders can be a liability rather than an asset. The challenge for women of faith today is to rest our own learning on an underlying biblical world view, recognizing that all of creation exists in relation to God. We need wisdom that integrates professional knowledge with spiritual depth. In our secularized culture, that is a big task.

We need those also who are committed to what is right. Even with the odds stacked against her, the wise woman of Abel Beth Maakah was no compromiser, but ready to be faithful to the truth as God revealed it. This continues as a challenge. I admire those Christian women in many different walks of life whose courage and compassion is evident in their refusal to compromise. Project Esher, in Christchurch, New Zealand, works with women struggling with abuse, facing hardship and serving prison sentences (sometimes after reacting to years of violation from their partners). Women's committed leadership can release and enable the lives of many others.

The wise woman of Abel Beth Maakah prevented the genocide of her people. Fundamentally, like Abigail, she was a peacemaker, committed to working against bloodshed and carnage. Today the need for peace exists everywhere – within families, at work, among neighbours and between nations. We know that reconciliation is always better than war. As followers of the Prince of Peace our calling to peacemaking will always remain central, whatever our situation and wherever we are.

Questions to ponder

1 What is your perception of King David's rule? What strikes you as outstanding in his leadership, and what do you think were his main weaknesses?

2 Some churches are committed to pacifism. Do you know which they are? Who are the peacemakers in your family or social circle?

10

Two mothers in
desperate dispute

1 KINGS 3.16–28

This story of the two mothers is mostly told to show the skill of King Solomon, son of David and Bathsheba. The human authors of the text clearly want to highlight his insights and discernment and we might think that the women are merely the foil for displaying those. But when we read the story at another level it is very much a women's story. It opens a window for us on motherhood. It lets us feel the emotional commitment of mothers to their offspring, and illustrates what it means to have unconditional love. Two mothers both face an unexpected and challenging dilemma, but only one of them deals with it as a true and loving mother.

The location of the events is a brothel. Once again, prostitution provides the background for a human issue. As prostitutes who lived and traded in the same place, the two women probably knew each other well. They would certainly have faced the same struggles and hardships common to many prostitutes, whose livelihood involves the sale of their bodies. In the course of their encounters with clients, both become pregnant (although in neither case are we given any information about the father). Pregnancy and child-birth would have restricted the opportunity for earning money, and this may have been resented. But it also would bring the joy of having someone they could really love. We can imagine that the two women shared their journey through pregnancy together, perhaps even enjoying the same experiences of new life growing within them. And so the nine months roll by, the time for birth arrives and a son is born to each woman within three days of each other.

But then tragedy strikes. One baby dies. An exhausted mother desperate for sleep unwittingly rolls on her off-spring and suffocates him. But which one? That becomes the all-consuming question. As one child lies lifeless, the women no longer share the joys of new parenthood but become adversaries. They are caught up in a fierce contest over the identity of the remaining live baby.

An appeal is made by one of the women to the king. It is inconceivable in our age that someone should have immediate access to the highest authority in the land to re-solve a personal dispute. It can't have been normal in these ancient times either, which is why some scholars suggest the story is more illustrative than historical. But, we are told, the women stand before Solomon, who takes on the case and listens carefully to the plaintiff.

The mother who brings the case is in great distress. Her allegation is that her baby has been kidnapped. She awoke to find a dead child beside her and was grief stricken. But in the daylight she realized quickly this was not her own son. It was the inert body of the other woman's son, who had been born some days after hers. She alleges that this other mother has swapped her dead child for the live baby, which is now happily suckling from her.

It was in every way a heart-rending situation. A dead newborn infant and a disputed offspring: we can well understand that the emotions of both women were running high. Possession, however, was even then nine-tenths of the law. The mother who had the live baby in her arms was not ready to relinquish him. Despite all the pleas and arguments of the other, she insisted that he was indeed her child, and staked her claim for guardianship.

Solomon might have been a wise king but he was not an obstetrician. Although he may well have had his own inkling, he was hardly qualified to establish, clinically, which of these babies belonged to which mother. And the ethnic characteristics were so similar. In fact, he appears to make no effort to arrive at any such decision, but instead gives a surprising order to his servants: 'Bring me a sword!'

Imagine what it must have felt like for the child's mother to witness what followed. As she listened to the legal process and adjudication, the humanity of her baby disappeared; he became nothing more than a material object. She must have gasped with horror as Solomon publicly began to apply the well-known law of dividing disputed property. She may have seen the result often before. If two people came to court holding on to a sheet of linen or clothing, each claiming it was hers, with no strong evidence to support either, the law ruled it should be divided. So the court officials would ceremoniously cut the cloth in two and each woman would be given an equal half. And now, to her horror, this same procedure was about to be carried out on her precious baby son. Surely this wise king did not really believe that the law of dividing disputed property could apply to babies as well as linen!

She probably didn't notice, however, that Solomon asked for the sword to be given to him, rather than to the officials who would have been commissioned to carry out the verdict. If she had, she might have guessed that he really had no intention of having her baby cut in two, but had another motive. Nevertheless, the king succeeded in convincing both women that he was serious.

The two women then faced the prospect of a second dead baby – one that would be brutally killed because of a dispute between them. Hearing the king's ruling, their emotions and responses were very different. The already-bereaved woman was motivated only by grief and anger. She had lost her child. She did not care if someone else lost hers also; in fact, it almost pleased her. With no sense of compassion for this defenceless, innocent offspring or his frantic mother, she readily agreed that the tiny child (whom she claimed was hers) should be cut in two.

For the other mother, her baby's safety and protection was the sole issue at stake. Motivated by love, she wanted simply to ensure his security. If the only way she could achieve that was to place him in the hands of this callous woman, it had to be done. We could almost hear the trembling in her voice as she withdrew her petition, pleaded for his life and agreed that he should be given to her rival. She was ready to let him go and to sacrifice her happiness for his safety. And, of course, in doing so, she was recognized by Solomon, and all the court, as the authentic mother. Her petition succeeded.

Facing our challenges today

This is really not a dilemma that would be faced by any mother in our culture today. Judges in our courts don't test the witnesses by making outrageous suggestions, and no one would propose chopping up babies! Yet there are many disputes over custody and it can be all too easy for parents at war with each other to use their child as a weapon against the other. The authentic mother in this story wanted only what was best for her child, even if that meant giving in to her rival's claims.

On a wider scale, many mothers today face challenges that revolve around issues of vulnerability. Our children today are susceptible to harm. That's why safeguarding measures have taken centre stage. Children can be exposed to bullying, grooming, abuse and peer pressure. Their vulnerability makes us anxious. Vulnerability is built inevitably into motherhood itself. It follows from love. Whenever we love another person deeply we become vulnerable, because the well-being of that other takes priority over our own well-being and even our security.

It's easy for a mother today to be confronted with a sense of powerlessness. The mother in the story felt powerless to bring about the result she wanted and just go home with her baby son. How many of us have felt powerless to bring about the results we want for our children? We want them to have kind friends, but see them facing nasty cliques that enjoy undermining or belittling them. We want our children to be confident in their own bodies, but we live in a culture that makes them feel fat or ugly or gender-insecure. We want our children to grow up well and fulfil their dreams, but feel inadequate to help as they struggle with failure and disappointment. Yet, in all of this, we know that mothers can give their children the one ingredient they need most – unconditional love. This alone reaches down through pain, anger or rejection to speak peace and safety into the hearts of those we cherish. However inadequate we feel as mothers, our love can produce miracles for our children.

One of the greatest tests of motherhood is also illustrated by this story: the need, eventually, to let go. This mother had little choice, for her son's life was at stake. She knew that life with her rival would be a horrible option for him, because she had already seen the disregard this woman had for his life. But at least he would live. And letting go enabled her to discard her own longings in order to preserve his life. Sometimes we have to let go in difficult circumstances, even with great reluctance. It can be heart-breaking when our children make decisions that we feel are bad. It is so hard for a mother to watch her child walk into a situation that she knows, in her maturity, leads only to a dead end. Yet none of us knows the future. Situations can change, life moves on and new opportunities open up. Mothers who have been able to let go, yet carry on offering support to their children, know that this is all part of parenting. For though we are guardians to our children, their lives are not under our control. God's role for us is to nurture, guide, educate, warn, admonish and build up our children, but not to dominate. Love offers a better way. When we are able to step back and place those we love into the hands of God, we may well learn that God's parenting is infinitely better than our own.

Questions to ponder

1 What is your response to Solomon's methods? Can you think of any other ways that the true identity of the mother could have been established in those days?
2 What do you feel is the saddest part of this story?

11

Huldah: speaking
truth to power

2 KINGS 22; 23.1–25; 2 CHRONICLES 34

If we had to conjure up an image of Old Testament prophets, we would probably see them predominantly as old
men on top of mountains, with long flowing beards and
raised arms. They're usually represented that way in paint-
ings, although Rembrandt had a more sensitive approach
and painted Jeremiah far more poignantly, weeping over
Jerusalem. But, however they are depicted, we inevitably
think 'men'! Yet seven women mentioned by name in
the Scriptures are designated as prophets in the Jewish
tradition. We've looked at some of them already – Miriam,
Hannah, Deborah and Abigail, but also included are Sarah,
Huldah and Esther. These women lived in different centuries. Not all of them were 'official' prophets in their day, but
each had powerful prophetic insights that were important
for her own generation.

Huldah, like Deborah, was a prophet recognized by the
people she served. She lived in the reign of King Josiah.
She was a descendant of Joshua bin Nun, which meant she
was also a relative of Jeremiah, the outstanding prophet
who prophesied in the streets of Jerusalem. We know of

Jeremiah because his prophecies are recorded in Scripture, as are those of Zephaniah, another significant prophet of the period. Although there is no 'book of Huldah', she had received the gift of prophecy as a young woman and was revered as wise and prayerful before God. In the biblical account, there is no suggestion that her status as a woman was any different from that of the male prophets.

Huldah's husband, Shallum ben Tikvah, was prominent in the royal court. He was the keeper of the king's wardrobe, which gave him responsibility for the king's robes and clothes on all occasions. Young King Josiah had inherited the throne at the age of eight when his father, King Amon, was murdered. This king had been a disaster for God's people, as had King Manasseh, his father before him. They had both turned their backs on God, embracing idolatry and pushing the nation along the road to destruction. Thankfully, young Josiah was advised differently by eminent teachers: Jeremiah, Hilkiah the high priest, Shallum and Huldah herself. They were all determined to help him recover the faithful God-fearing tradition of his great grandfather, King Hezekiah, who had set the benchmark high for kingly rule. Under their wise teaching and influence, Josiah rejected the idols that had littered Judah, going out with his men to break and destroy them. Then he began the task of encouraging his people back into obedience to God.

In the eighteenth year of his reign (c. 621 BC), the young king launched a massive programme of national renewal. As part of this, he undertook the huge task of restoring the long-neglected Temple in Jerusalem. He called a mass rally asking people to participate in this great undertaking. The response was enthusiastic; contributions for the work of restoration poured in. Josiah sent his secretary to instruct High Priest Hilkiah to give money to the carpenters, builders and stonemasons, who needed to buy the materials and dress the stone ready for rebuilding. Spirits were mounting. Honesty and integrity were to become the watchword of the restoration, and the place was once again to become the centre of worship and prayer.

In the middle of the bustle of new work, a totally unexpected event occurred. A missing scroll of the Torah was found in a secret hiding place. This scroll had originally been kept in the holy of holies in the Temple, but had been removed for safe keeping during the long periods of idol worship. Hilkiah's thorough management of the work was rewarded: the precious parchment was uncovered and sent to the king. We can imagine the huge excitement in the palace at the news, and then the utter fear and dismay when the scroll was opened and its contents read.

The scroll opened at the section in Deuteronomy where God warns the Jewish people of the terrible consequences of neglecting the Torah and turning away from faithfulness to God. They would face destruction and exile. King Josiah knew his father and grandfather had desecrated the holy land with idolatry and evil. They had burnt incense and bowed down to stone statues. They had dedicated their horses and chariots to the sun god. They had even sacrificed their children as burnt offerings on the altars of Molek. Tearing his clothes in mourning, he sent Hilkiah, along with four other royal messengers, to ask the prophets for immediate advice. He needed to know if the disasters spoken of in this authentic text could be averted in any way.

So where did the messengers go? We might have expected it to be a choice between Jeremiah and Zephaniah. In fact, they went to neither. They went to the prophet Huldah. Given the dire warnings in the scroll, they had to hear what God's intention was for the people and the nation. They trusted Huldah's prophetic insight and waited in anticipation for her response.

For Huldah, this posed an issue indeed. The challenge was not whether she understood what was written in the scroll. That was plain for all to read; it was indeed the Law of God. Neither was the challenge to know what God was saying to the people. Huldah was a wise prophet and had been gifted powerfully in discernment and understanding. She could certainly interpret the word of the Lord with integrity and authenticity. No, the challenge was how to find the right words to deliver the devastating news of God's anger towards his people, and his deep rebuke at their unfaithfulness. She had to bring an indictment against the kings of Judah and to deliver it to King Josiah himself.

It is quite likely that the messengers were hoping that Huldah would tone down the harshness of these words from the Law. It would be comforting if she could find some indication that because these things were in the distant past they no longer mattered. But Huldah did not. She knew that time does not wipe out sin, but a price will always be paid, at some time, for wrongdoing. Yet when evil is not faced and met with repentance, its effects can continue through generations. She knew too that only God can forgive, not the passage of time. Change is ushered in through penitence before God and through hearts that ask for forgiveness.

And so Huldah spoke words that must have been almost unbearable to hear. The penalty for idolatry and wickedness would visit the nation. Disaster would fall upon the people, and the land and those who lived in it would be laid waste. Evil would be rooted from its midst. The catalogue of predictions was overwhelming. Yet, for those present, there was some good news. It would not happen in the reign of Josiah. God recognized that this king had chosen righteousness and grieved over the actions of his forebears. Because of his response to God, Josiah would not see the calamity that would befall the people but would live and die in peace.

When Huldah's prophecy was brought to the king, he was in no doubt at all about its importance. He immediately ordered the elders of Judah and Jerusalem to summon all the people to the Temple, where he read to them the words of the scroll. They heard, with their own ears, the divine warning, followed by the covenant that Moses and all the Israelites had made with God. Then the king renewed this covenant for himself and the entire nation, undertaking 'to follow the LORD and keep his commands, statutes and decrees with all his heart and all his soul'. The people responded, and undertook to renew the covenant fully.

So Josiah and Hilkiah began to clean up the land of all idolatry with its abominable customs, burning anything relating to Baal, Asherah, Molek or any of the other idols. A Festival of Liberation announced freedom from the slavery of idol worship, and a spirit of repentance, holiness and purity filled the entire nation.

Huldah's prophecy came true. King Josiah reigned for a further 13 years, but the destruction of Jerusalem and of the Temple came after his death. Huldah did not have to witness the terrible destruction she had foretold either. The prophet Jeremiah was the one to weep over the fall of the holy city. But Huldah's prophecy and influence remained as an everlasting inheritance for the people of Israel.

Facing our challenges today

The commission laid on Huldah, of having to bring appalling news to the nation's ruler, is personally known by only a few women. But the qualities reflected in her life and character are displayed by many others. Huldah was known to be a woman of God. People trusted her integrity and spiritual insight, and she drew them into the presence of God. She did not court popularity, was not motivated by a need to be liked, but was secure in her relationship with God. Consequently, she felt free to speak truth to those in power, whatever it might cost.

Today, we are challenged to manifest these characteristics. We're confronted by the need to be women known for our trustworthiness and consistency, whose integrity is upheld by what we do and say. These are becoming rare commodities in our culture. Yet if we don't stand against the slide into moral relativism or inertia, our witness as Christians will be marred. We are challenged to resist the temptation simply to affirm or flatter others to gain popularity, but to be honest and truthful in what we say. We are confronted by the demands of exposing things that are wrong, rather than sweeping them under the carpet out of indifference, fear of authority or rocking the boat.

We can be challenged today by other women who show the qualities of Huldah in the way they speak truth to power. Exposing the corruption of tyrannical leaders, many brave women across the world denounce hypocrisy and warn of the moral bankruptcy of injustice. In many countries the future of children, trafficked victims, enforced child brides and even female foetuses in the womb have depended on the words of women activists who call law-makers to account. In a post-truth age where lies flow easily, we all need the courage to speak out and build bridges so we can work together with those who oppose evil. As Christians, we know that all our initiatives have to be surrounded by prayer because to take a stand for justice might have dangerous repercussions. Yet we must accept the challenge Huldah faced, of speaking the truth in love. In the era we live in, it could be one of our greatest tests of faith.

Questions to ponder

1 Does it seem strange to you that so many of the kings of Israel and Judah turned out to be idolaters and bad rulers? What do you feel is the reason?
2 Why do you think there are few sermons on Huldah in churches today?

NEW TESTAMENT WOMEN

As we move into these next stories, we need to remember that some four hundred years elapsed between the last of the Old Testament documents and the earliest New Testament writings. Much changed during this period, which was to be reflected in the challenges that the women faced. Geopolitical changes, the sacking and rebuilding of the Temple, and changes in the regulating of religious observance, all mark shifts that occurred during the intertestamental period. Inevitably, they provide the background and context for most of the stories we shall read.

In the Hebrew Scriptures, the Israelites were contending with the Assyrians, Babylonians, Persians, Egyptians and others. They were persecuted and taken into exile, then a remnant returned. By the time of the New Testament, the Greeks had defeated the Persians and invaded Palestine, bringing their language and culture with them. Whereas

Jesus would have learnt his Scriptures in Hebrew with some Aramaic, the whole of the New Testament was written in Greek.

Graeco-Roman culture was now dominant and the relationship between the pagan Greeks and God-fearing Jews was not always easy. Jewish groups like the Essenes grew up, and nationalist surges like the Maccabean revolt gave the Jews a time of independence. By 63 BC, however, the Romans had entered the fray, conquering many lands and taking control of Jewish territory. The Roman Empire was vast and Roman rule affected the lives of everyone, including Jews and Christians. In the first century BC, Pompey conquered the eastern Mediterranean, including Palestine, and Julius Caesar conquered Gaul. Julius Caesar was assassinated in 44 BC, and successive Caesars each left their mark, through enforced taxation, military dominance or the eradication of dissidents. Several of them – Augustus, Tiberius and Claudius – are named in the New Testament, and its political historicity is evident. The emperors allowed local kings to rule over the territory the Romans had captured, but in Palestine Herod the Great was cruel and brutal, even to his own people. The Synoptic Gospels' account of Christ's nativity is set in the context of his ruthlessness.

Worship was very significant in the Hebrew Scriptures. Centuries before, the First Temple, built by Solomon, had replaced the tabernacle (Deuteronomy 12.2–27), but it was sacked by the Egyptians some decades later. It was partly rebuilt, and then completely destroyed by the Babylonians in 586 BC. After the fall of the Babylonian Empire, a Second Temple was begun. Completed after 23 years, it faced many attacks and lootings, right into the intertestamental period. Around 20 BC it was rebuilt and expanded by Herod the Great and became known as Herod's Temple. This was to feature in many of the Gospel narratives.

Instability, Greek and Roman dominance and political repression were thus set to provide the background for some of the women's stories. One key aspect of culture, however, had remained constant throughout those four hundred years: the underlying patriarchal nature of society. Now it was more than a familial structure where authority was vested in the male tribal leaders; it was a structure reinforced by the patriarchy of imperial Rome, traditions in the Temple and the growth of new religious authorities and institutions. During the intertestamental period, synagogues had grown up, with the management of worship carefully regulated and monitored. New Jewish groups had emerged, like Pharisees, scribes and Sadducees, none of which were obviously present in Old Testament times. They flourished from 165 BC to the destruction of the Temple in AD 70. The Sadducees were an elite, priestly class, with legalistic interpretations of the Torah, whereas their opponents, the Pharisees, were largely lay-led. Although in fundamental disagreement with each other, between them they exercised strong religious control, refusing to relax the restrictions that had grown up and reinforcing the subservient status of women. Their legalistic interpretation and enactment of the law would barely have met the approval of the prophets in the Hebrew Scriptures, and was also an ongoing source of rebuke from Jesus. It is significant in the account in John's Gospel (chapter 8), where Jesus is asked by the Pharisees to adjudicate in the stoning of an adulterer, that they bring only the woman before him. Yet the law in Leviticus 20.10 made it clear that it applied equally to the adulterous man and woman. Women's freedom was thus doubly impeded by the outlook of these authorities, and Jesus' challenge to them in John 8 is well noted.

In the Hebrew Scriptures, women's assigned domestic role gave them dignity and wide responsibility, as evidenced in the praise of the competent woman in Proverbs 31. Later, the Pharisees increased women's participation in worship, giving the lighting of the Sabbath candle to the mother of the family. In the New Testament Gospels and Epistles, women were not honoured for their domestic roles but for their faith. They were included in leadership, and in Paul's great statement of Galatians 3.28 hierarchies of gender, race or status dropped away in the body of Christ. The stories of the women in the pages that follow share a unifying theme. They are all told against the background of Christ's messianic identity, prophesied in the Hebrew Scriptures and consistently referred to throughout John's Gospel. And it is in his encounter with two of the women in these stories that Christ's identity is explicitly revealed. In the 14 episodes I have chosen from the New Testament, each of the challenges that the women faced had some connection with the cultures in which they were located, but they were also woven into the underlying narratives of Christ's teaching, healing, death and resurrection. The background and experiences of these women are different. The stories are specific to them. But the possibility of liberation and new life is the melody that accompanies them all.

12

What Mary said when the wine ran out

JOHN 2

John's Gospel makes quite a feature of the wedding at Cana. As in most eras, weddings were great celebrations, occasions of congeniality and lavish hospitality. We don't know where this wedding was, but the indications are that it was in a vibrant, busy community, where families lived close to each other and knew one another. Archaeologists have identified Khirbet Qana, 8 miles north-west of Nazareth and 12 miles west of the Sea of Galilee, as the most probable ancient site where the wedding took place.

We have no idea whose wedding it was, or how many people attended. But we do know the guest list was inclusive. Mary the mother of Jesus was present, as was Jesus. The disciples had also been invited. It is more than likely, too, that Jesus' brothers and sisters would have been there, older ones perhaps bringing families of their own. It appears that the hosts had extended a welcome to many people to celebrate and enjoy the marriage festivities for as long as they continued. In some cultures this could be for hours, even days, so we can guess that huge amounts of food and drink would be needed to keep the guests happy. Killing a fatted calf would have been no exaggeration.

As a guest, Mary clearly had no responsibilities for this lavish hospitality, yet it is clear that when the crisis came she shared some of the anxiety of those providing it. The eating and drinking was well underway when Mary picked up the muttered conversation between the stewards and hosts. The wine had run out. There probably had been just too much thirst to quench. To run out of wine in a wedding celebration was no small faux pas. It was a major social embarrassment, little short of an insult to the guests. And although few people seemed yet aware of the problem, it would soon become very evident as the crowd of guests sat around, waiting for the servants to serve more drink.

It appears that Mary was on close terms with those throwing the wedding banquet, for she saw it as her responsibility to help. She experienced immediate empathy for the bridegroom and his family; their humiliation would have been intense. So she did what she would probably often have done in her own family routine: she turned to Jesus. John briefly records her observation, quite likely no more than a low murmur: 'They have no more wine.'

What was Mary expecting of Jesus? It was clear that her comment was intended to do more than pass on information and indicate her concern. Jesus himself certainly interpreted it as more than that. She was trying to involve him in finding a solution. But what was she asking him to do? It was unlikely that he would be able to go and buy the amount of wine needed for the guests, and it certainly was not a 'bring a bottle' event. Jesus had not, at this stage, become publicly identified with producing miracles, yet Mary seems to have known something that others didn't. Whatever she was asking, it seems that she believed implicitly that Jesus could save the day for the wedding hosts.

Jesus' own response to her has been the subject of much speculation. 'Why are you trying to involve me? My time is not yet come.' This has even been interpreted by some as being something of a family joke: Jesus pointing out that he's not the bridegroom, so his time to take responsibility for restocking wedding wine hasn't come yet! This idea is not unlikely. We can imagine that there was often teasing and banter between Mary and her sons. Yet phrases very similar to this occur in different places in the Gospel of John ('my time is not yet' comes three times in chapter 7) and they usually indicate something more serious. Each time, Jesus seems to be pointing to a direction set for his life, where God's own timing will overrule current situations. But each signals a pause, for that time is not yet.

Whichever way we hear it, however, Jesus' reply to Mary does not sound to us to be very hopeful. With regard to the looming social crisis, it sounds like a very definite 'no'. And in most situations that would be the end of the matter. There would be no more wine, people would be offered water, and there would be some disappointment and disapproval. For ever afterwards, that wedding would be remembered partly for its inadequate hospitality. But what happens next is somewhat extraordinary. Mary completely ignores Jesus' implicit refusal, takes the matter into her own hands and starts instructing the servants to do whatever Jesus tells them to.

There are few, if any, incidents in the Gospels where Jesus is overruled by family or friends. He more often rebukes them for not understanding that he takes his authority from God and not from human beings. On another occasion, when Jesus is teaching and someone brings a message that his mother and brothers are outside, he dismisses this, insisting that his mother and brothers are those who know the word of God and keep it. Here, however, having first implicitly refused, he falls into complete compliance with Mary. He orders the servants to fill the huge ceremonial water jars with water and then serve some to the chief guest. Water was itself a luxury in a parched land, and few would refuse it, even if disappointed. So, no real surprises there. The surprise was that when this guest drank the water it had become wine. The hosts and stewards 'in the know' must have been astonished. Not only had the hospitality crisis been averted, but Jesus had enhanced the celebrations with luxury and abundance. The chief guest's warm compliments to the bridegroom ('you have saved the best wine until now') affirmed the generosity and fullness of the miracle.

It is fairly clear what Gospel writer John wants us to learn about Jesus from this incident at the wedding. It is that Jesus cares about people's material needs as well as their spiritual state. He has concern for the whole person and the whole community, bringing the reality of God's love into the everyday-ness of people's lives. But more than that, John wants us to see Jesus fulfilling signs that he is sent by God; he has power and authority over the elements of the earth; the very water is his creation. Jesus is the abundant miracle-maker in whom the glory of God is revealed.

Mary's part in all this is very significant. She has had many challenges since an angel first appeared to her and told her she would give birth to a child. She had then been involved in an arduous journey while pregnant, a precarious delivery, the search for a missing son at the age of 12 and constant anxiety over his welfare. Far more challenges were to come. But the angel had called this child the 'Son of the Most High', and she has glimpsed many times what that might mean. At this time of joy and celebration, it is no surprise, then, that her awareness and initiative bring into action Jesus' first miracle.

Many aspects of Mary's character stand out in this story. It's clear that she was directed towards the welfare of other people. This gave her a level of shrewd observation towards details. She wanted the wedding to go well and, like many women, she put herself effectively 'on guard' to identify any potential problems. In fact, had she not seen the impending predicament, the outcome might well have been very different.

Second, she had prophetic insight. She knew the Hebrew Scriptures and saw in her oldest son the embodiment of the messianic hope that all Israel had been waiting for. She had nurtured him, watched him grow into adulthood and knew him well. Despite what Jesus said to her, she knew his ministry was about to begin. Of course, she could not have known this was how it would start, or where it would go. But she was confident it would be a ministry of blessing and healing.

She also had enormous trust in Jesus. She knew, instinctively, that he would respond to the crisis with generous love from God. Producing the very best wine from basic water didn't only save the face of the hosts. It also replaced their poverty with God's abundant riches and enabled them to use their resources to bless others.

It is also obvious that she was audacious in her confidence. To hear Jesus disavow the task she has put before him, yet still instruct the servants to do what he says, gives us a glimpse of her assurance that she rightly understood the will of God. She believed that God wanted to bless the start of this young couple's married life and encourage the families, and that Jesus was the one who would bring God's will to fruition. She met the challenge with faith. She interceded with her son, spoke authoritatively to the servants, and left Jesus to do whatever he would.

Facing our challenges today

Often, in our time, we wish that we had Jesus with us in body so we could call on him to exercise miraculous power. Inevitably, our experience of Christ is different from that of Mary. Yet many aspects of her attitudes and reactions are helpful to us in the way we grow in faith today. We can learn from her own boldness and trust, that Jesus is willing to work with any of us, in both mundane and global contexts. We can pray meaningfully into the most difficult areas of the world. Whether it's the fundamental challenge of providing food and shelter for the dispossessed, the need to combat climate change or to contest the build-up of war, we can call upon Christ's help and guidance. For we know we are working with the vision God gives us for humanity, not against it.

We can learn from Mary's confidence that prayer puts us in deeper contact with God's love. Mary's comment to Jesus was a prayer that she did not need to repeat or build up, but simply needed to leave with him to bring whatever outcome was right. We too can intercede for people in situations where others might simply shrug their shoulders and say things are impossible. But we know that, even when the odds are stacked up high against a different outcome, God can intervene and change things.

Mary's empathy was a valuable gift from God. The ability to experience the pain of others, to feel their distress, is a gift in short supply. For their pain becomes ours, and most of us would rather not have extra emotional burdens. Yet Mary had empathy in abundance, and her later suffering would become great. Today, God still gives the gift of feeling to those who ask. When we too stand alongside others in need, God can use us to bring encouragement and hope, so they know that the crisis is never too big to bear.

We don't have to elevate Mary as the mother of Jesus to appreciate what she has to teach us. For, like us, she was human and subject to the same frailty and weaknesses. But we can allow her realization that God is in Christ, reconciling the world to himself, to shape our own outlook. And we can receive her prophetic insight into Christ's saving and healing power as part of our lives also. At the very least, Mary's story can inspire us to face, with faith, whatever the future has in store.

Questions to ponder

1 What do you think old Simeon meant when he prophesied to Mary at Jesus' presentation in the Temple that a sword would pierce her own soul?

2 What do you think might have made Jesus reluctant to get involved in this problem of hospitality? Can you think of other instances where people's material needs became his own concern?

13

The Samaritan woman who broke the stereotypes

JOHN 4.4–30, 39–42

I don't know many stories in the New Testament that have been as badly retold as that of the encounter between Jesus and the Samaritan woman. I first came across it in my teens. The ardent preacher pointed out in no uncertain terms that this woman had made a complete mess of her life. She seemed unable to form lasting intimate relationships and had broken up with five husbands. With each new marriage she probably vowed that she would do better, but no, it always ended in failure. And now she had given up on marriage altogether and was 'living in sin'. No wonder she didn't want to be questioned by Jesus and said she had no husband. She even tried to divert Jesus from probing her past, with an irrelevant question about where we should worship.

That seemed to be the common interpretation. Yet getting into the story years later, with rather more background knowledge of life and culture in that first century, the penny dropped. This was no restless, dissatisfied woman, deliberately hopping from husband to husband. In that patriarchal culture women could not divorce their husbands; husbands divorced their wives. When Jesus insists on limiting grounds for divorce (Matthew 19.3–9) it is against this background. He wants to protect women from being discarded for no good reason. This particular woman had probably first been married while young to an older man. He had either died or divorced her and she had subsequently become wife to a sequence of men (possibly in the same extended family), and in each case her marriage had ended. Now, her current partner hadn't even married her, so she was in a cohabiting relationship with no legal protection. When we realize how vulnerable and socially isolated this left her, probably with problems too of low self-esteem, the whole story begins to make much more sense.

John's account is very specific. The woman comes to draw water from the well at noon and she is alone. I preached on this passage in an African village church, where the women's roles were uncannily similar to those in the New Testament context. I asked the women if they went to the well at noon. They laughed at my question. Of course not; that would be pointless! The household needed water from the very beginning of the day. They went to the well at 6 a.m. So, did they go alone? They laughed again. No, they all went together, with their sisters, cousins, mothers and neighbours. 'Why?' I asked. Well, obviously they needed to look after one another, to make sure no one fell and help draw water for those who were pregnant or elderly. Their early morning communal walk to the well was a happy, sociable routine.

The Samaritan woman in the story went to the well,

alone, in the heat of the day, to avoid the time when the other women were going together to get water. She knew she wasn't welcome in their company. And as a 'discarded woman' she didn't want to be an object of scorn, pity or suspicion from the others.

So it must have been a huge surprise for her to find someone else at the well at that time – a Jewish male no less. I would imagine that her instincts would have been to turn round and go back, except that Jesus spoke to her. This in itself was odd, but what he said was extraordinary. Slumped by the well, tired and thirsty, he asked her for a drink. For a Jewish rabbi to make himself so vulnerable to a Samaritan woman was unheard of. Layers of prejudice, prohibition, disdain and discrimination were loaded into the Jewish–Samaritan relationship. Her reply showed she understood it well.

Her concern was not that the request was demanding for her, but that it was demeaning for Jesus. Jews had no dealings with Samaritans and, anyway, she knew the no-contact rule, the ablution laws and the need to purify vessels. If Jesus were to accept a drink from her, he would need to go through stringent purification rituals so that his drink would not be contaminating. Yet Jesus brushed aside her concerns and began to talk about the *living* water he could give her. An amazing conversation followed. It covered eternal life, ancestry, her past marriages, Jewish–Samaritan differences and the place and nature of worship. She learned there were no restrictions, whether imposed by Jews or by Samaritans. God did not need people to be in temples or on mountains to praise him, for God can be worshipped anywhere. In fact, during their time together, Jesus shared with her some of the deepest spiritual realities about God. Why? Because Jesus saw the heart of this woman rather than viewing her as others did. To him, she was not immoral, an outsider or of no consequence. She was intelligent, trusting and a faithful seeker after God's truth.

Though confused at first, the woman slowly understood. Her words, 'I know that Messiah [called Christ] is coming. When he comes, he will explain everything to us', conveyed her sudden realization that Messiah could in fact already be with her. And Jesus quietly confirmed it: 'I, the one speaking to you – I am he.' In one of the few episodes mentioned in the New Testament, Jesus disclosed to her his messianic identity. (On another occasion it was again to a woman – Martha.)

The rest of the story is equally exciting. The woman forgets all about drawing water from the well and becomes a different person, throwing off fear and reluctance to face other people. She rushes back to her neighbours and urges them to come and meet Jesus. Her own encounter with Jesus has transformed her into an evangelist. Her words are so persuasive that her neighbours don't hesitate to follow her back to the well. Within the space of meeting him, they confirm for themselves that Jesus is indeed the Anointed One (John 4.39–42).

The challenge for the woman in this story is not an obvious one. She is not asked to find courage, defy authorities or take risks. She is asked simply to let go of her past and see herself in a new light. Jesus negates the way her culture sees her and invites her instead to understand God's call on her life; she can worship God anywhere, in spirit and in truth. And in grasping that, the woman also recognizes Jesus and is transformed.

Facing our challenges today

This woman's story challenges each of us to reflect on who we are and what holds us back from knowing the power of God in our lives. We might have problems with insecurity or trust. There might be things we want to leave behind us, but don't know how. We might have a history that we are not proud of, a past record we would rather rewrite: bad decisions, perhaps, or actions that have harmed other people, which we now deeply regret. We might be struggling with old hurts, rejection, abuse or betrayal. We might even still experience trauma when these memories come up for an airing, or flashbacks we can't control. All of these leave scars, often very deep ones, which need to be healed in our lives.

The past inevitably creeps into our present, insisting, insinuating and demanding to be heard. C. S. Lewis once commented that past sins cannot be resolved by time, but only by the blood of Jesus. It is a very wise observation, which Lewis himself found to be true. We can also apply the same maxim to past damage that has never been repaired. That too can be healed by the power available through the blood of Jesus.

Yet there is often a journey to be made before we arrive at this point. We might first have to recognize our *need* for healing; be ready to move from denial to truth as we let ourselves go into those areas we have put out of bounds. We might have to face the bullies in our lives, or those who put us down, and begin to know our worth in the kingdom of God. We might have to see ourselves not as others see us but through the power of God's love.

This woman's life changed through a 'chance' encounter with Jesus at a well. We too are invited to encounter Jesus. That is why prayer, meditation, penitence and forgiveness are so central in the Christian faith; they draw us into an ever-deeper walk with God. God knows our past as clearly as Jesus knew the life history of the Samaritan woman. And we can only ultimately let go of the hold that the past has on us by facing it together with Jesus, placing it in the hands of God and asking the Holy Spirit to release us.

When we do that, we can be confident that where we need to forgive others, God can give us strength. Where we need forgiveness ourselves, Christ's love can set us free. We don't know what the outcome might be in our lives. But we do know that, like the Samaritan woman, we can walk into the future with new hope.

Questions to ponder

1 Why do you think Jesus made himself vulnerable to the Samaritan woman? And why did the woman react, initially, as she did?

2 What aspects of your own past might you need to leave behind?

14

A most embarrassing party

You are at a garden party with some well-known celebrities and have just sat down to eat. Your discreet gathering is sectioned off from the general public, but people are milling around close by and are quite free to stop and look across the barriers. Without warning, an uninvited woman rushes over and starts to make physical contact with one of the high-profile guests. She takes out a jar of aroma oil from her bag, and starts kissing the guest's feet and giving them a massage. When she unpins her long hair, one of the other guests mutters that she is a local prostitute. You feel rooted to the spot with embarrassment, wondering what on earth will happen next.

This incident, related in Luke's Gospel, must have had a similar impact on the guests at the meal in the house of one of the Pharisees. The only person who seemed untroubled was the one at the centre of the encounter: Jesus himself. When the other guests began muttering and doubting his discernment (and probably his morality), he remarked rather pointedly that their own hospitality had been somewhat lacking. They had not given him water to wash his tired feet or welcomed him with an embrace or anointed his head with oil. But the woman had made up for their lack by her generous expression of gratitude towards him.

Who was this woman? There are accounts in all four Gospels of a woman anointing Jesus, sometimes massaging his head, sometimes his feet. In the accounts in Matthew, Mark and John the stories are similar. The location is Bethany and the topic of conversation around the table is the money 'wasted' on the extravagant use of the oil, when it could have gone to the poor. In the Gospel of John, the woman is clearly identified as Mary, sister of Martha. But in Luke the story is different. The location is the Pharisee's house, the unnamed woman is described as 'a woman of the city, a sinner', and the topic of conversation is about forgiveness and love.

So many questions confront us about why this woman took on the challenge of disrupting the party and lavishing this physical affection on Jesus. Why was she there watching the meal in the first place? What was she doing with a jar of expensive, luxury oil in her possession? What drove her to disregard stringent religious and social protocol to make physical contact with a rabbi? And how did she know that Jesus wouldn't rebuff her?

We can piece together some of the answers. Jesus' reputation had spread and it is likely that this woman had already had some experience of his teaching and healing. She probably knew he was to be at the Pharisee's house and had come along, wanting to see him. What she saw, however, must have saddened her considerably. As she gazed at his dusty, tired feet she would have been very aware that Jesus was not being given the warm welcome and bodily comfort due to him. Although he had been invited, he was more of a trophy than a person. Little affection or consideration for any tiredness was shown him. It seemed clear to her that he was not wanted for himself but simply for the benefits he would bring his host. If the woman was indeed a prostitute, she could easily identify with that. Men wanted her, but not for herself, only for what she could do for them. Her actions towards Jesus speak of her deep empathy with him.

Rushing over to Jesus may have been an impulsive act, but it could also have been driven by a desire to compensate for the poor treatment he was receiving from his hosts. It is interesting that the focus was on Jesus' feet. Feet are not usually the part of the body that we lavish attention on. In a hot, dusty climate with lots of walking, they might well have been smelly and off-putting. This woman was not put off. She kissed them, wet them with tears and dried them with her hair. Hair was regarded as a woman's glory, but she was using it as a foot towel. The fact that she lavished expensive oil on them also seems significant. As a former prostitute she might well have used such oils for her most wealthy clients. It is as if she were bringing her former trade to Jesus and, quite literally, laying it all at (and on) his feet!

The other guests are not impressed. Their muttering about Jesus' discernment is audible. Instead of asking the host to have her removed, Jesus addresses the issues they voice. Yes, the woman is a sinner; her debts are many. (In that sense, of course, she is no different from the party guests, or us. We all have many sins.) Then Jesus tells a story about the release of debts, asking the guests a question about who is likely to love more. The answer is that those who are forgiven much love much, and this is illustrated by the forgiven woman's compassion towards Jesus. But those who are forgiven little love little. So, by implication, in their absence of love, the host and his guests show they know far less of what it is to have their sins forgiven.

Most of those gathered at the meal see the woman as an offensive and unwelcome intruder. Jesus sees her as a role model for a forgiven life. To the annoyance of the others at the party, he commends her for her faith and releases her from any remaining weight of sin, to go in peace. The question left on everyone's lips is, 'Who is this who even forgives sins?'

I wonder if the woman had any idea of what would happen when she burst in on the party. I suspect not. The challenge for her was simply to show Jesus how much she appreciated him, and pour out her love in a practical and intimate way. But in doing so, she raised, for everyone else, the question of their standing before God. She walked away in peace, knowing she had blessed Jesus. She walked away in freedom also, knowing that she was through with the past. The weight of memory, pain and moral defeat could be put behind her, and her new life had started. But what of the others at the party? Most of them were far behind, because they had not yet recognized they needed to take the first step. While they lived in self-delusion and self-righteousness they would not experience the joy of release from sin.

Facing our challenges today

Acting in a way that brings public attention to themselves is a very big challenge for people who are shy or reserved. The average introvert would usually rather just merge with the crowd. Even extroverts would have to think twice before conducting a performance like this! But, sometimes, God might ask us to step outside our comfort zone and do something unexpected, as a witness to his love.

I was on a tram in the city of Sheffield when I was aware of some embarrassment and panic among fellow passengers. Looking down the carriage I realized a Christian evangelist was going from seat to seat, politely offering to pray for people. The people opposite me were terrified. Most people shook their heads, but the Christian, a black woman aged around 30, was undeterred, smiling: 'God bless you.' Then someone said quietly, 'Yes, I would like prayer. I'm going to have an operation tomorrow.' The woman sat with her, raised a hand over her head and prayed God's healing and blessings into her weary body. People stared, not knowing how to react. The woman expressed thanks. Realizing how uncomplicated prayer was, two other passengers suddenly accepted the invitation. Prayer broke out. Despite the prevailing scepticism, the atmosphere in the tram began to vibrate gently with the power of God's love.

Like the woman in Luke's story, the tram evangelist also knew what it meant to have her sins forgiven, and she wanted to bring the love of Jesus in any way she could for others to experience. She reached out to them with prayer because she knew that Jesus is the source of hope and love. This conviction can often lead Christians to go against the cultural norm and do the unexpected without fear. I have sometimes seen the most shy and reserved people transformed into those able to offer a public witness to the God who loves them. The greatest difficulty is to take the first step.

The biggest challenge of the story, however, is to allow God to search our own hearts and show us where we need help. Living with denial about the past keeps us locked into it. Refusing to face our faults causes us to repeat them. Acknowledging what was wrong before God is the beginning of a new future. Reaching out in repentance and knowing the power of forgiveness starts to release us. It gives us the ability to make amends towards those we might have hurt, or to let go of resentment towards those who have hurt us. As this woman powerfully shows us, it is so much better to leave those weights behind and walk free.

Questions to ponder

1 What made the woman so unafraid to pay such attention to Jesus in public? Do you think she had thought about it beforehand, or were her actions simply impulsive?

2 Some people get more satisfaction in resentment and bitterness than in forgiveness and restoration. What might hold you back from seeking reconciliation with people who have wronged you, or making amends to those you might have offended?

15

Joanna: well connected but surprising

LUKE 8.2–3; 24.10

One of the aspects of a patriarchal culture is that women are subsumed under the category of 'men'. They don't count on their own. So when Luke names women who were followers of Jesus, we know he is breaking the patriarchal mould. One of the women he mentions is Joanna.

The women who accompanied Jesus on his travels were no less significant than the male disciples. We can assume that they each had their own call from Jesus to follow him. But whereas Jesus largely invited the 12 men to be followers as they were doing their normal work, the call to the women was different. In some cases it seems to have come through an experience of healing. It is unsurprising perhaps that Luke gives us this information, for, as a doctor, he had a particular and professional interest in healing. Joanna is mentioned along with Susanna and Mary Magdalene as someone who was cured of 'evil spirits and infirmities'. However, unlike Mary's problem, which is specifically cited in terms of deliverance, we don't know anything about the nature of Joanna's healing. We don't know what her infirmity was or what brought her to Jesus.

We do know, however, that she became a devoted follower of Jesus, so the initial encounter must have been powerful. From that time on, she wanted to be in his company and share somehow in his ministry to other people.

We need to understand the significance of this mixed group of itinerant followers. It was unusual and counter-cultural, to say the least. The Jewish rabbis taught that women should not even socialize with men who were not their relatives, much less travel with them. In fact, Jewish men were discouraged from having any substantial discourse with women outside the family. Jesus was acknowledged as a rabbi but, in disregarding such traditions, clearly welcomed Joanna and the other believing women as his companions on the journey.

If it was unusual for single women to be in Jesus' group of followers, it was unheard of for married women to be following a roving rabbi. Joanna stands out as someone who broke with tradition on a number of counts. She was married, yet seemed to spend little time at home on duties prescribed for wives. Even more, she was married to an important official, and her absence would surely have been noted by many people in his orbit.

Luke describes Joanna in relation to her marital status, in keeping with accepted protocol. She was 'the wife of Chuza, the manager of Herod's household'. Her husband was a palace man; no run-of-the-mill officer, but someone entrusted by Herod with many of the key aspects of domestic management; most translations call him Herod's 'household manager'. So this immediately raises a very interesting question. What was the wife of a man busy with the affairs of the Galilean king doing following an itinerant rabbi rather than supporting her husband in his role, and maintaining her own domestic responsibilities towards her household? We don't know. Curiously, we are not told whether she also fulfilled her domestic roles, or whether she simply left her husband to cope as well as he could. Yet it was so abnormal for the wife of a high-up official to be wandering around towns and villages with a teacher and his disciples that we must wonder what Chuza made of it.

There are some clues to this in the situation itself. First, it would not be normal for a married woman to go absent without leave, so we can assume that Chuza knew where she was and that she was travelling with Jesus. In fact, if this had been any kind of defiant act towards her husband, she would not have been his wife for very long! A patriarchal society did not encourage men to tolerate independence in their wives and made it relatively easy to divorce them. So we can assume she had her husband's support for the way she spent her time.

Second, we know that Joanna supported Jesus financially, and possibly the disciples also (Luke 8.3). Luke records that the women gave out of their own means, which implies that Joanna had her own income, either independently of her husband, which was unlikely, or through his sharing income and wealth with her. Again, it would have been unusual for a man to give his wife a free hand in the way she spent their resources, and this too suggests that Chuza both trusted Joanna and respected her decisions.

This is not a husband, then, who was threatened by the

fact that his wife was deeply committed to another man! It is far more likely that Chuza recognized Jesus as someone very special. Far from being a competitor for his wife's affections, Jesus was the one who had restored her and brought healing and new life. What could be more natural than for Joanna to want to support his ministry so that others could be blessed too? I suspect that she would have had the full backing of her husband. If all this is true, we have an extraordinary reversal of patriarchal values and a strikingly liberated marriage. We are seeing a married woman who experiences extraordinary freedom in Christ, released by a husband who loves and supports her. Of course, Chuza might himself have experienced the good news of the kingdom of God, and become a follower of Jesus.

Nevertheless, Joanna risked social disapproval by associating with Jesus and the apostles. Whether approved by her husband or not, her lifestyle would have been anathema to the religious leaders of the day. Her challenge therefore was to hold together her Christian discipleship, her marriage, her domestic responsibilities and her generosity, without bringing either herself or her husband into disrepute.

We suspect she succeeded in meeting this challenge because we encounter her again in the final chapters of the Gospels. We can see that she has remained committed to the vision that Jesus imparted, and to serving him personally. When Jesus is tried, condemned and executed she still follows him. She seems unafraid of letting her total allegiance be known. By now, one of his male disciples has betrayed Jesus, and another has denied knowing him, but Joanna stays firm. Along with all the other women who have followed Jesus from Galilee, she is faithful to the end. Her last gesture of love will be to anoint Christ's body in the tomb.

Facing our challenges today

In many churches across the world today there are still pre-scribed roles for wives. I was struck when doing research on violence against women how often men, even churchgoing men, saw it as their entitlement to govern their wives and require them to fall into line. Some even saw it as permissi-ble to beat their wives if they disobeyed. The combination of a controlling autocratic personality and distorted theology can be a toxic blend. Women married to such husbands find they are not only 'walking on eggshells' (as one of them confided to me) but can be worn down by abuse. A report, published by Restored in the UK in 2018, *In Churches Too: Church Responses to Domestic Abuse – a Case Study of Cumbria* (edited by Kristin Aune and Rebecca Barnes), makes for very uncomfortable reading. It displays a sad portrayal of some of the abusive and restrictive treatment of women even in homes of churchgoers. The fact that two thousand years ago we have this startlingly liberated ex-ample of a married woman free to follow Christ suggests we need to question some of our own presuppositions about wives and husbands.

We need to ask why Jesus' challenge to patriarchal atti-tudes and control has still not filtered down in some areas of the Church two thousand years later. Far too often, the culture of a church uneasily reflects the culture of the society in which it is placed. In reading the Bible, they have reinforced the patriarchy of those days rather than the liberation offered by the vision of God's kingdom. And although we can find Christ's radicalism about gender mirrored in churches throughout Christian history, these have often been groups that have broken with the mainstream in order to liberate their women.

How we follow Christ is the key theme in Joanna's story. Traditionally, women who publicly followed Christ set aside everything to join religious orders. They took vows and chose celibacy over marriage and family life. Their daily and weekly routine was set by requirements of meditation, worship, community life and work. Over the centuries this has declined, with a huge drop in women taking religious vows in Europe and the USA since the 1980s. In the USA, Catholic nuns have declined by more than 72 per cent over 50 years, and the average age has risen to around 70. In the UK, whereas there were 80 new nuns each year in the 1980s, only 7 entered a convent in 2004. Other traditions had gained ground – Protestant women becoming ordained ministers, charismatic women becoming worship leaders or prophets. Yet, in the last decade, more women have found their vocation again in religious orders. Forty-five entered a convent in 2014 and many chose to work in their profession as public Christians sharing convent life.

The desire of Christian women to follow Christ faithfully will always present challenges. Women who have family and work responsibilities often find they need to avoid being swamped by the daily demands made of them so that prayer and other Christian priorities are squeezed out. Women in professional life often find that they are regarded with amusement or scepticism if they declare their faith. Yet the call to be a full-time mother/scientist/doctor/ business manager *and* a full-time Christian remains. Ultimately, it is a matter of underlying perspective and attitude, so that the focus is on life commitment to God and not simply time allocation.

Questions to ponder

1 Most Christians take their biblical understanding of marriage from Ephesians 5. How does Joanna's marriage fit that pattern?

2 Why does it seem significant that the only financial supporters of Jesus named in the Gospels are the women in Luke 8?

16

When the bleeding had to stop

MARK 5.25–34; LUKE 8.43–48

Any woman knows that when menstrual problems set in they can be very limiting. It's not just the pain, and weakness from constant loss of blood. It's the havoc it can play with our social life. For the woman in this story the issues were more extensive even than that. The patriarchal culture she lived in compounded the problem and provided few resources to overcome it.

We don't know the name of this woman. That's not surprising because she wasn't in the disciples' circles of family and friends, nor did she seem to be a person of particular renown. She suddenly appeared in the narrative as Jesus was passing through her locality. He was on his way to the home of a synagogue leader, whose daughter was dangerously ill. Jesus paused in fulfilling what others would have seen as a culturally acceptable request to allow a much more undesirable encounter. It brought up all the negative attitudes in Jewish culture towards women and menstruation. So, if the biblical authors did know who she was, they didn't disclose the information to us. Perhaps they were simply exercising discretion and allowing her some measure of anonymity?

We do know a good deal about her circumstances,

however, because Luke, doctor that he was, noted the details for us. She was likely to be approaching middle age, since she had been struggling with erratic and persistent bleeding for 12 years. She must have suffered enormous discomfort and dragging pain, along with that awful draining of energy which any woman with long-term period problems knows only too well. And she now had few financial assets because she had spent all that she had on trying to find a cure. If all this was not enough, she would also have been socially isolated.

The isolation was not simply a result of her illness or poverty, however. It was also because of strict religious taboos about women's menstrual blood. Contact with other people during a woman's menstrual cycle was strictly regulated, so this woman could well have been confined to her own living quarters for most of the time. We know this, simply by reading Leviticus 15.19–33. In fact, all the laws relating to menstruation in that passage give us a strong indication of the limitations of her lifestyle. She would have been ceremonially 'unclean' for as long as the bleeding persisted, and anyone who had physical contact with her would also be 'unclean' for the rest of that day. Anything she had been lying or sitting on would be seen as unclean and must not be touched by others. Even after the bleeding stopped, she would have had to wait seven days before she could be seen as 'clean'.

Her very presence among others was, therefore, a persistent hygiene problem, a religious conundrum and a legal risk. For someone in her situation, with such erratic and persistent flows of blood, there would be barely a gap between the bouts of bleeding. As a result, she faced no way out of this horribly restrictive cycle. Her chronic gynaecological problems, along with the attitudes of her culture, denied her any enjoyment of regular close company or a normal social life. So we can understand why she was desperate to see an end to her menstrual distress and had spent so much time and money trying to get better. When it was all to no avail, the big question was what to do now? To that, there seemed no answer.

If Jesus had not been in the area, the story might well have ended there and we would never have heard of this woman. But he was in the area, and the news of his whereabouts had reached her. Knowing of some of the other amazing things that had happened when people made contact with Jesus, she was suddenly filled with hope. Perhaps her own ailment could be healed and she could move into an entirely different future. First, however, there was a big problem to overcome. She had to find the courage to go out in public in her condition and ask this Jewish rabbinic teacher for help. And she had to do this despite the taboos laid out for her by her religion. She would have known that if she was detected in Jesus' company she would completely disrupt his journey by making him 'unclean'. Any contact from her would require him to change his clothing and go through ritual ablutions before he could travel any further. She would also have known that she herself would be subject to penalties for having violated the law.

Yet the woman was determined. She would not be held down by this crippling condition. So she formed a plan. She would mingle, unnoticed, in the crowd and not even try to speak to Jesus. She believed that if she could just get close enough for a few seconds and simply touch the bottom of his tunic as he passed by, his healing power could reach her. Then she could melt quietly away again and no one would be any the wiser.

We know that although the first part of the plan worked brilliantly, the second did not. Certainly, she got as far as the hem of his clothes, and was able to bend down, unobserved, and make contact. And, wonderful joy, she felt the effects immediately in her body. Without warning, the bleeding stopped. What had been an act of ritual contamination had triggered an outcome of amazing healing. We can imagine the enormous rush of euphoria. But it was short-lived because of what took place next. As for the plan of her quietly melting away, that certainly didn't happen.

It is interesting that it was Jesus who prevented the silence and anonymity when he asked, 'Who touched me?' With his divine discernment he would surely have known who had touched him without putting her on the spot. His disciples were also confused at his insistence. They might have interpreted this as his desire to know if indeed he had come into contact with someone ritually unclean. Characteristically, they pointed out that there was no way of knowing who had touched Jesus since the crowds were pressing in on him from all directions. Anybody could have brushed against his clothing. Jesus, however, remained persistent. It became clear that this was not because of any violation of the hygiene laws – he seemed indifferent to that. He raised the question because he knew someone had been healed. He wanted that person to identify herself.

The woman's terror at being forced out into the open was completely understandable. Her cover had been blown, and in normal circumstances her defiance of the laws could have had serious consequences. We can imagine what it was like for her to be 'trembling with fear'. She felt completely cornered. Sooner or later she would be detected. There was no other way out than to throw herself down on her knees and confess: a gesture of submission before the authority of a religious leader.

The remarkable difference in this story is what happened next. The fact that she got no rebuke from Jesus, no sharp criticism for having 'contaminated' his clothing or compromised his journey, must have surprised both her and the whole crowd. Instead, Jesus affirmed the woman, ignored the legal infringement and commended her faith! He made it clear that he approved of her taking the initiative. He even called her 'daughter', a reminder that her identity was not defined by law but by trust. She was indeed a faithful Jewish woman who worshipped God and honoured his will. In replacing her fear with peace, Jesus made it clear that she brought her own healing into play, through her trust in him.

In effect, Jesus brought together the polar existence of this woman. He redefined her identity from that of victim and outsider to who she really was before God. It was an identity that she already knew in her own heart, but which had been denied her by her culture's legalism. She had the courage to keep on claiming her own authentic identity, believing that Jesus could confer it.

Facing our challenges today

We can learn so much from this woman on how to face the debilitating things that challenge us. Her story gives us both practical and spiritual insights. Her disability was overwhelming, but she refused to be defined by its limitations. There was nothing more she could do to find a cure, but she could still reject the attitudes of other people and the restrictions those attitudes placed on her. She could still move forward in faith and not be dragged down into hopelessness. She was determined to find a new purpose for the future. In this story, she received physical healing from Jesus. Some of us have experienced physical healing that we know is from God. Many others of us can be brought into different kinds of freedom where God can bless and renew us.

All patriarchal cultures offer severe restrictions on women, mostly far worse than those in this story. Some make women subject to male 'guardian permission' with regard to what they may do, or where they may travel; others coerce girls into female genital mutilation or child marriage, leaving them with a future of pain or educational deprivation. Yet others collude in the sexual violation of women and offer little legal redress. I believe it is the responsibility of Christians in all cultures to reach out across the globe and support initiatives working to end these restrictions and bring women's empowerment. Keeping in touch with organizations like 28 Too Many, Girls Not Brides or Karma Nirvana can keep us informed and enable us to play our part.

Those of us who feel trapped and held down by much

more mundane things can also be encouraged to find the strength to move on. We can refuse to let our fear of others restrain us from what we know to be right before God. We can reject being sucked into hopelessness, and start working instead on the steps we might take to break the chains that keep us in bondage. We can ask God in prayer to widen our horizons so we begin to see the opportunities that we miss when we focus on our despondency. We can actively experience the energizing of the Holy Spirit as we step out in faith.

Healing and empowerment take so many different forms in all our lives, for we face circumstances that are specific to ourselves. But they often begin when we recognize, as this woman did, that however vulnerable we feel, we are never alone in the challenges we face. When we confront them in faith and hope, we become more able to understand what else God might yet have in store for us. We need never lose heart. For even in the worst and darkest parts of our lives, we can find that God's grace is sufficient for us and that Christ's strength is made perfect in our weakness.

Questions to ponder

1 Why is women's menstrual blood seen as negative in the Old Testament text, whereas men's circumcision blood is seen as positive?

2 Why do you think Jesus forced this woman out into the open when she was afraid of what she had done?

17

A Canaanite woman: sassy, and full of faith

MATTHEW 15.21–28

The encounter between Jesus and the Canaanite woman has puzzled readers of the Gospels for centuries. Why does Jesus appear so indifferent to a woman desperately anxious about her daughter's mental state, and treat her with such disrespect? And why does the woman persist when seemingly given very little encouragement?

In fact the encounter is a turning point in Matthew's account of Jesus' ministry, and this woman is far more significant than we might first think. The context is that Jesus has been experiencing growing hostility from Jewish religious leaders and is now moving out of their territory into the Gentile region of Tyre and Sidon. He has performed an amazing miracle, feeding five thousand hungry people, and will go on to feed four thousand more following this encounter. But in between these two miracles comes this strange story.

Matthew's Gospel does not name the woman but lets us know that she is a Canaanite. In fact she is the only person in the New Testament who is described in this rather old-fashioned way. (Mark simply refers to her as a

Greek, born in Syro-Phoenicia.) Matthew's reference will have meant much more to early biblical readers who knew Jewish history; they will have known that the Canaanites were ancient enemies of the Israelites. Centuries before, when they were to enter the promised land, the Hebrew people were told to destroy the Canaanites rather than make any treaty with them. They were to show them no mercy, for the land was given over to idolatry and there must be no risk of idolatry compromising Israel. Yet idol worship did continue among the dwellers of Canaan, and the prophet Zephaniah was later to issue his warning to them: 'The word of the LORD is against you, O Canaan, land of the Philistines' (Zephaniah 2.5). So the woman in this encounter is a descendent of some of the oldest idolatrous opponents of Israel.

Nothing in the woman's manner indicates this, however. The opposite is the case. Three times she calls Jesus 'Lord', which is the way his disciples and followers themselves address him. It is a far more reverent and devotional title than 'Rabbi', which is how the scribes and Pharisees and many of his enemies address him. She also refers immediately to his Jewish status – 'son of David'. Jesus has entered her geographical territory, but she receives him on his own cultural and theological grounds. She makes it clear that she accepts their difference and knows that, morally, she has no claim on him; all she wants is God's mercy.

The response of the disciples, nevertheless, is immediate: 'Send her away!' And at first, Jesus seems to concur. He ignores her and points out to them he has come to the lost sheep of the house of Israel. This in itself, of course, is hardly a claim for Jewish superiority. People of Israel are 'lost' and need to find God again. The woman hears this too, but rather than being put off she takes it as encouragement. Even though Jesus is sent to Israel, surely she can still be included in his ministry. So she kneels before him in worship and pleads for her daughter to be restored. Jesus' next response is even more discouraging. He says it would not be right to give the children's food to (little) dogs. Yet still she refuses to be fazed. Her response is full of logic and full of faith. She points out, in effect, that the 'little dogs' are ready to lap up the scraps that the 'children' reject.

It is a clever response. I wonder if she might even have been familiar with Jesus' parables, because he refers in them to the destitute and needy longing for food scraps from the privileged. In the story of the rich man and Lazarus in Luke 16, for example, Lazarus was 'longing to eat what fell from the rich man's table'. In the parable of the prodigal son (Luke 15), the son far from home was even prepared to eat the pods the pigs were eating. Whether she did or not, her response touches a chord in Jesus. Clearly moved by her reply, he remarks that her faith is great and, because of this faith, her daughter will indeed be healed. It has echoes of his response to the woman with menstrual problems. He turns the focus away from his own power and on to the woman's strength of commitment.

This account is one of 14 individual healing miracles in Matthew's Gospel. And it has many parallels with the story of another 'Gentile' healing: that of the centurion's servant (Matthew 8.5–13). Both stories feature a Gentile who is seeking help for someone they care for, and in each case the humility and trust of the plaintiff is in marked contrast to the arrogance and denial of Jesus' opponents. The healing takes place at a distance, simply through the promise of Jesus, without his entering their homes, and the supplicants are commended by Jesus for their great faith. The fact that they are not part of the 'lost sheep of the house of Israel' demonstrates that Jesus' ministry is already becoming global.

An interesting development seems to confirm this. In her reply to Jesus, the woman has opened up the link between feeding and healing. And this link then continues after they part and her daughter is healed. Going up a mountain near the sea of Galilee, Jesus becomes quickly surrounded by the crowds who need him. He heals their sick and, when they have been with him for some days, goes on to produce another 'feeding' miracle. This time it involves four thousand people, and seven basketfuls of leftovers are collected at the end. Matthew makes a point of saying that the crowd 'praised the God of Israel' (Matthew 15.31), which probably indicates that they were not Israelites themselves. The biblical scholar R. T. France suggests that this second miracle may well have been for a Gentile crowd. The woman's response to Jesus can be seen as almost prophetic. The food that he offers is sufficient to feed both the 'children' of the family and all those outsiders who believe in him.

What is surprising about the woman is that she had the nerve to approach Jesus at all. In those cultures (and in many today) women didn't talk to strange men in public. Even more, a woman from a racial minority did not initiate a conversation with a Jewish rabbi. It would have seemed highly presumptuous and courted dismissal. The other surprising thing is that she was not offended by Jesus' initial rejection, or of his choice of words in his provisional reply. She was able to see through these barriers to the truth that Jesus embodied, and this kept her going. Despite his first calling being to serve the Jews, she somehow knew his mission was much greater than that. And in her reference to dogs eating scraps she indicated she was willing to accept whatever might be on offer, and do it on his terms. The result was that Jesus clearly admired her gutsy rejoinder, and his ministry was opened up by her response. The woman from Canaan received not simply crumbs from the table but all she could have hoped for; her daughter was healed.

Facing our challenges today

Many commentators see this story as Jesus testing the woman to find out how serious she was about her need of him. We might ask this of ourselves: are we serious about our faith, or merely lukewarm? Does our need for Christ come somewhere below our need for a nice house, good friends or a well-paid job? This woman's need was ultimate. She knew the debilitation that had gripped her daughter, and that only Christ had the power to restore her. This poses a question churches often reflect on today: do we believe that *our* hope is founded on Christ alone?

This woman's faith enabled her to continue, even when she might have felt put down. This is another challenge. We usually find it hard to ignore negative comments from other people. Many of us can take offence very easily. Especially when we hear something that sounds demeaning or insulting, we can respond in anger or go off in a huff. This woman offers us a cleverer strategy. Rather than taking umbrage, she returned the objectionable comment with a wise and challenging riposte. She turned what could have been an insult into a smart quip. It's a good way forward. When we can work positively, or even playfully, with an otherwise offensive remark, we stay focused on the central issue rather than allow ourselves to be distracted into defensiveness. And we are more likely to defuse the situation that way. We retain the mental energy to make our points clearly to others and achieve a much better result. Jesus probably didn't need to be persuaded to go beyond the borders of Israel to spread his kingdom. It was all in God's plan. But his timing might well have been influenced by the conversation with this woman.

We saw how the Canaanite woman did not allow the limitations placed on her by society to affect her relationship with Jesus. It is a very important stand to take. Across the world today, women are challenged not to let the limitations on them mar their relationship with God. We should resist anything – age, gender, class, education, poverty, disability or even distorted theology – that holds women back from experiencing the power of God's love in their lives. Whether we are women in patriarchal cultures, Christians in Islamic/Hindu/Buddhist cultures, or black women in white-supremacy cultures, God gives us the freedom to worship him in spirit and truth. And we must work together to ensure that the freedom God gives is not taken from women by systems of repression.

Questions to ponder

1 What parallels do you find between Jesus' encounter with the Canaanite woman and the one with the Samaritan woman? In what ways are they different?

2 When Jesus opposes any hint of racist superiority, why do you think that we still struggle with racism in the Church? Do you have any examples of this, and how it can be overcome?

18

More to the widow than her mite

MARK 12.38–44

Supposing we saw a thin, elderly woman in threadbare clothes, shuffling past a collection box at the back of a church. She stops, looks at the box, then takes out her purse and empties everything she has into the box. What would we feel? Horrified? Worried that she had dementia and didn't know how to look after herself? Some of us might even rush up to her and say, 'No, you don't have to give all that. That box is for people who've got money to spare.' We might even start asking around about where she came from or phone the social services.

When a poor widow in the Temple does just that, Jesus' response is very different. He uses her as a role model, focusing on her integrity and unselfishness. He contrasts her with others giving money and points out that she outdoes them all. It isn't the size of her offering that he acclaims but her motivation and what it costs her. Her giving fulfils the central command he has already outlined; that we should love the Lord our God with all our heart, soul, mind and strength, and our neighbour as ourselves. And it costs her everything.

The woman was poor and a widow. The two very often went together in patriarchal societies. Women were largely dependent upon male relatives – fathers, husbands, brothers, sons – to provide for their well-being. This didn't mean they didn't work. Younger widows would be busy journeying to the well to fetch water, making and selling things in the market, or working in the household of a relative, yet with minimal income from their efforts. Older widows would prepare food and look after families; in some cases they might have sole responsibility for grandchildren if their own son or daughter had died.

The plight of widows was well acknowledged in the first century. Concern for them had been reflected for generations in the social and economic code of the people of Israel. As long ago as the time of Moses, the law had made special provisions for the poor, especially widows. The gleaning laws, for example, stipulated that farmers were not to harvest their crops to the edge of the field, or go over the harvest a second time (Leviticus 19.9–10; Deuteronomy 24.19–21). This meant that some easy-to-reach crops were left unpicked so that widows, orphans and destitute foreigners could all go and help themselves. Then the tithing laws required wealthier people to bring their excess crops to a central store every three years, so that grain and stocks would be available for this same group of poor people (Deuteronomy 14.28–29). The Temple, especially, was a place where these laws should be honoured. By the time of Jesus, these provisions were still in operation.

However, the vulnerability of widows was not always respected, and this adds significance to the woman's generosity.

For the incident in the Temple is in a much bigger context. Just before Jesus draws attention to the widow, he has been making serious allegations against those with religious power. They are hypocritical, self-interested and don't look after the people. Several allegories are there in the text, like barren fig trees and vineyards that produce no fruit. The Pharisees, Herodians and Sadducees all suspect he is telling his parables against them, so attempt to discredit him. Yet even though they hurl a series of questions about taxation, marriage and heaven, Jesus continues to expose their hypocrisy, and the crowds love his wise answers.

The scribes are next for attention. Jesus warns his disciples that the scribes are corrupt; they enjoy pomp and status but they take the best for themselves. They devour widows' homes, exploiting them rather than offering support. Worst of all, they do all this under the pretence of prayer. Their actions deny the truth of what they profess. These are powerful indictments.

This all provides the context for Jesus' comment to his disciples on those giving to the Temple treasury. He notes that the wealthy can afford to give, but the widow is vulnerable and her sacrifice is even more poignant. Her dire poverty is a reflection of the hollowness of the faith of their leaders. She has not been cared for. The Temple system has not provided her with means of support. She now has nothing left. And yet she still gives.

The generosity of this widow is thus in enormous contrast to the corruption of the religious establishment that Jesus exposes. She is not simply a role model of generous giving; she is also a role model for true belief and worship.

Her devotion to serving God reaches into every part of her being. She doesn't parade her spirituality, but quietly worships. She doesn't hold on to money for herself in a fearful, clenched fist, but opens her hand to release it, so that God's purposes might be fulfilled. Although she has so little, she holds nothing back, in marked contrast to the religious leaders who have much, yet take for themselves. Her actions echo the call given to believers in the book of Ecclesiastes (11.1): 'Send out your bread upon the waters, for after many days you will get it back.' She implicitly trusts that God is no one's debtor and what is given away in God's service will be returned in some form or other. In fact her action anticipates Jesus' own teaching: 'Give, and it will be given to you. A good measure, pressed down, shaken together and running over, will be poured into your lap. For with the measure you use, it will be measured to you' (Luke 6.38).

It is not surprising therefore that Jesus invites us to reconsider where to go for our understanding of faith and all its implications. It is not to the religious teachers and officials, leaders, who make a mockery of worship, but to this poor widow, who loves God. The double outrage was that her sacrifice was not being honoured by those called to steward gifts, for the Temple was not fulfilling the purposes of God. So, along with commendation of the widow, Jesus issues a warning to the false teachers (Mark 13.2). Judgement will come and the Temple itself will be razed to the ground. Not a single stone will be left standing. And though his warning was to religious leaders of his day, the same need for integrity surely applies to leaders at any time who claim to speak with the authority of God.

Widows are significantly highlighted in the New Testament. Sometimes they are the focus for individual attention. Anna, a widow for over 50 years, is in the Temple when Jesus is being dedicated, and prophesies over him. The widow of Nain loses her only son and Jesus brings him back to life. The early followers of Jesus are urged to make the care of widows a priority and not to discriminate against them. The importance of treating widows properly is highlighted particularly through a dispute in the book of Acts. When the Greek-speaking Christians complain that their widows are not receiving the same benefits as the Hebrew widows, the apostles come up with an immediate solution. They set up a group of deacons, many of whom are Greek, to oversee fair distribution of resources and make sure all the widows are properly cared for (Acts 6).

Caring for widows was a mark, then, of true belief and brought people close to the very heart of God. Believing widows had much to teach others about the commitments of faith. Despite her poverty and the indifference shown to her sacrifice by religious leaders, this widow who gave her all was rich beyond measure in the economy of God.

Facing our challenges today

We are challenged on so many levels by this story. It is often used predominantly as a case study for generosity. Are we mean-spirited in our giving, always calculating our own needs and wants first, before we consider others? Or do we give with abandon, not counting the cost but responding compassionately to need, and trusting that our gifts will be used wisely? We know what the answers are, even if it is more difficult to apply them consistently in our lives.

The widow's example is often used too to urge us to be free from anxiety. We don't have to worry about the future because it is in God's hands. We can respond in prayerful faith to the needs around us without being able to predict the future, for trust, rather than fear, will help us to live much freer lives. These important insights need to be at the forefront of our stewardship of money and gifts to help direct the policies of our churches and organizations.

Today, many ethical principles in the New Testament are being opened up in relation to the current management of money and resources. Principles like not going into debt, making proper provisions for the well-being of our families, earning our keep, not over-consuming, not being a burden on other people and supporting the household of faith are woven into the morality of Christian stewardship. Many of us have learnt these things and practise them daily. We take responsibility for the financial care of our children; we share what we have with others; we support Christian organizations that care for the needy or marginalized; we give support to elderly folk who need our time and help; and we cut back on waste and our carbon footprint. We are learning in our world today that the planet's resources are finite and God's creation should be honoured and not wasted by negligence or indifference.

Yet, other principles are not followed through. We often seem afraid of challenging corruption in our culture and the waste of valuable resources because it seems beyond our remit as Christians. We don't probe the 'donations' given to our public leaders by people with vested interests. We don't make a fuss about the disparity of rich and poor in areas of taxation or benefits. We don't campaign for more resources to go to poorer areas of our own country rather than to richer areas, because it all feels a little political. Jesus did challenge the systems of his day and the religious rulers who benefited from those systems, for they violated the fairness and compassion of God. Holding leaders to account for how they exercise integrity and treat the poor is surely part of our own calling as Christians.

The poor widow is a role model for so many of us: for those of us who are rich and can well afford to give, that we might be more generous and give with abandon; for those of us who are poor or anxious, that we might trust God in ever more areas of our lives. She is a role model for the pattern of discipleship: not giving to impress others or to get approval, but giving to God alone, knowing that God sees the motivation of our hearts.

God knows us and sees what other people so often miss. He sees the values we live by, the struggles we encounter and the sacrifices we make, and receives the gifts we bring. God is for us, always ready to forgive us, bless us and make our lives more fruitful. But we are here also as Jesus' ambassadors, to bring good news to the poor and set captives free. It could be that, even in our age, this widow challenges us to be advocates for those who have no voice.

Questions to ponder

1 What motivated those in power to disregard the weightier aspects of the law? What were they?

2 In what ways does this broader reading of the widow's mite encourage us to go beyond simply affirming generosity? What areas of injustice today might it inspire us to take on?

19

Martha knows what she believes

JOHN 11.1–44

'She's such a Martha!' I've heard this description more than once meted out to some woman or other who feels everything lies on her shoulders and wants some help from others. Quite apart from showing very little empathy for a woman under pressure, the comment is not really fair to the original Martha.

We all know the story of Mary and Martha. It is in the context of an event at their home. Their esteemed friend, Jesus, is teaching, while in the background food is being prepared for the crowd of people assembled there. Mary, the younger sister, is happy to leave her older sibling to do all the preparation and catering for the hospitality. She is caught up with the other disciples, absorbing the teaching and wisdom Jesus is sharing, and seems oblivious to the fact that meals don't prepare themselves. When Martha, in sheer desperation, appeals to Jesus to intervene and send her sister to the kitchen, he refuses. He points out that Mary has made the right choice, and that Martha shouldn't get so worried and upset about ordinary, mundane things.

Thousands of sermons must have been preached on this passage, most of which see Martha in a bad light. Sermons about spiritual priorities, our need to learn, making the most of time with Jesus, or warnings against self-pity, all compare Martha's preoccupation over routine with Mary's keenness to be with Jesus. Some see the issue as Martha's obsessive domesticity; others see it as her unkindness in attempting to undermine her sister before Jesus, rather than gently asking her for help. But, however it is interpreted, we learn only negative things from Martha.

So it comes as a surprise when we see a very different Martha in this passage in the Gospel of John. The context, now, is a sad one. Their much-loved brother Lazarus has died, and Jesus failed to arrive at Bethany in time to heal him. Of course, this in itself is odd. The Gospels record that Jesus was quite capable of healing people at a distance without even seeing them. We've already noted that he healed the Canaanite woman's daughter whom he didn't know and had never met. Lazarus and his sisters, on the other hand, were good friends. What's more, having decided to go to Bethany following the sisters' message, Jesus then deliberately delays his journey. So, he chooses neither to heal in person nor to give healing from afar. When he does finally arrive, Lazarus has been in the grave for four days.

And, this time, Martha is the one who rushes to be with him. The family house is full of well-wishers from Jerusalem, and Mary is with them, but Martha sees Jesus approaching outside the village. She has probably been looking out for him for days. Both sisters are devastated by their brother's death and deeply hurt by Jesus' apparent indifference. But Martha had been the one to nurture young Lazarus after their parents had died, and she loved him almost with a maternal love. Now at last she sees Jesus. Her longing for his help, along with her own good manners and hospitality, dictates what she must do. She leaves the crowd of mourners and runs out of the village to join him.

The conversation between Martha and Jesus is intriguing. It begins, unsurprisingly, with a rebuke from Martha: 'If you had been here, my brother would not have died.' She certainly needed to get that off her chest. In many ways she is no different from the psalmist who expressed many rebukes towards God for not intervening in a desperate situation. But then she adds a tantalizing challenge: 'But I know that even now God will give you whatever you ask.' What was Martha saying? What did she want Jesus to ask for? Did she really believe that Jesus could bring Lazarus back from the dead?

Jesus' assurance that Lazarus will rise to life again gets Martha's agreement. She is a believing Jewish woman and readily acknowledges that there will be resurrection on the last day. But then comes the most overwhelming claim from Jesus: 'I am the resurrection and the life. The one who believes in me will live, even though they die; and whoever lives by believing in me will never die. Do you believe this?' Martha is confronted by one of the breathtaking 'I am . . .' declarations in John's Gospel. And Martha's affirmation – 'Yes, Lord . . . I believe that you are the Messiah, the Son of God, who is to come into the world' – has resounded through history. Like the Samaritan woman at the well, Martha reflects back her faith in the messianic identity of Jesus. So whatever previous impression the Gospels might have given us of Martha, her real character is underlined by this profound, earth-shattering statement of faith. She knows with every ounce of her being that Jesus is indeed the Son of God, and one anointed by God, and that he has power over life and death.

The rest of the story is well known. Mary joins them both and repeats the rebuke to Jesus for his lateness. Jesus, moved by her tears, weeps himself over the sorrow and brokenness of death. Going to the tomb, and followed by the crowds, he asks that the stone across the entrance be rolled away. Characteristically, Martha points out that the body will smell! Practical woman that she is, she cannot help but attend to domestic details. She has to be reminded by Jesus of their earlier conversation. Then, with dramatic authority, Jesus calls Lazarus out from the dead, and to the utter amazement of the crowds the man is restored to life and reappears among them. The final symbolic action is the removal of his grave clothes, so that Lazarus is freed from everything that places him with the dead and not the living. Alive again, he is reunited with his sisters and resumes his place at Bethany. Martha has met the greatest challenge of her life with trust in Jesus and it has been vindicated.

Martha is presented in the New Testament as a complex character. She is preoccupied with routine and the mundane, but is also a person of great faith and trust. She takes her responsibilities very heavily and is often weighed down, but she's also full of insight and vision about what God can do. Many women vacillate between extremes like these. We can't always get it together. But Martha accepts her complexity and doesn't beat herself up over it. What she shows us, supremely, is that when it matters most, the faith that God gives can open us up to the central truth that Jesus is Lord, and that can affect every area of our lives.

Facing our challenges today

The way Martha faced her two huge challenges resonates today. First, she had to cope with unbearable loss. So many of us face that challenge, perhaps even right now. Loss is one of the hardest burdens to bear, whether it's the loss of someone we love or some other kind. Loss of sight, hearing, fertility, health, mobility or youth all makes its impact. Even the break-up of a relationship, redundancy at work, or moving away from friends can leave us with a gaping chasm in our lives. And loss is not something we 'get over' in the way we get over flu or a bad cold. It is something that becomes absorbed into our lives and forms part of our ongoing identity. Loss changes us; it can even wound us, and leave us broken and fragmented. If we don't seek peace in our experience of loss, it can turn into bitterness, which eats us alive. Martha took her loss to Christ, and the miracle happened. When we take any loss to Christ a miracle can happen for us. Most of us do not seek the raising of the dead, but we can long for the reality of knowing God's presence in our sadness, and a deep sense of his love for us. And the miracle can be the ushering in of fresh hope and greater purpose for the life that remains.

Martha's second challenge was bound up with the first. It was how to cope with apparent indifference to her pain from Jesus, the one she believed in. This challenge to

Martha is common to anyone who experiences disappointment in God. Disappointment can fill us with doubt and anger, where we want answers to the persistent question, 'Why?' When this trauma was not necessary and produced no good results, why should I have had to go through it? Lament in the Psalms, however, shows us that disappointment can also be part of believing. It was *because* Martha believed that Jesus was the Son of God, who answers prayer and brings healing, that she felt let down. If she'd had no faith, she would not have been disappointed. And for many of us who know that God can heal, but find that God doesn't heal for us, a blow to our prayer life and our trust in God seems inevitable.

The steps Martha took out of this have something to teach us. She is ready to encounter Jesus, even though she is hurt. She does not run away from him, or refuse to open up. Instead, she is real with him, speaks words of blame, rebukes him for his unresponsiveness, shares with him the pain in her heart. With us too, God knows how we feel and can take our anguish and anger without offence. When he sees the sisters' grief, Jesus weeps. In a world where sin and brokenness are part of our human life, the tears of Jesus remind us that he has trodden this way also. He is not immune to sorrow in the human heart, but he has come, as Isaiah prophesied, to bind up the broken-hearted. And those of us who reach out to God, ready to expose our hurt and misery, can find that God shares our suffering and pours his love into our grief. Even in our grief and distress, the Holy Spirit can show us the rainbow in the storm, and begin to help us to experience our life anew.

Questions to ponder

1 What aspects of her relationship with Jesus enabled Martha to speak the truth to him about her pain? How was his response to her helpful?

2 Is there loss in your life that you have not yet been able to process and fully accept? What holds you back from giving it to God and finding ways of moving on?

20

Pilate's wife: God challenging through dreams

MATTHEW 27.19

History often records the names of men who were significant in the past, while their wives remain nameless. This is true of Pontius Pilate's wife. All we really know of her is in one small verse in the Gospel of Matthew. Yet that single verse has inspired volumes of literature and has given the wife of Pilate a special place in some Christian traditions. Origen, an early Greek father of the Church, maintained that Pilate's wife became a Christian after Jesus' resurrection (although we don't have historical evidence for this). The Orthodox Churches have even produced a name for her – Procula or Claudia – and she is revered by many of them as a saint.

Other writers, however, suggest her role was more negative. This comes out in the medieval York mystery plays when she is regarded as a potential threat to God's plan of redemption. They suggest that Satan was trying to use her to prevent our salvation through Christ's death on the cross. We have twentieth-century interpretations also – most of which give her a much more prominent role than the single mention in Matthew's Gospel. She crops up in

Dorothy L. Sayers' radio play in the 1940s – *The Man Born to be King* – where she is referred to as 'Claudia'. In Sayers' script she meets the woman whose daughter has been miraculously healed, hears Jesus' teaching about himself, and witnesses his triumphal entry into Jerusalem. A very dramatic moment in the play is the death of Jesus on the cross. Pilate's wife remembers her dream, and prophetically hears a chorus of voices chanting what will become part of the creed: 'He suffered under Pontius Pilate.'

We might ask why a woman mentioned so briefly in one verse of Scripture has inspired so much imagination in literature and tradition. One answer is, of course, the context. Jesus was being condemned to death, and her husband had the sole means of preventing an unjust sentence. So anyone who played a part in his decision was important. But Pilate's wife herself captures our imagination. A determined woman, she boldly attempted to intervene in the affairs of a forceful state. She tried to sway her husband's verdict in a highly sensitive trial brought by religious leaders who resented Roman rule. Acting on a powerful dream, she proceeded with absolute certainty against her husband's vacillation.

As Roman governor of Judaea under the emperor Tiberius, Pontius Pilate had a difficult task. Since the Roman overlords were in charge of the occupation of a foreign state, they were hardly going to be popular among the Jewish leaders. According to the historian Josephus, Pilate's style of leadership didn't help matters. He was authoritarian and prosaic, taking away many privileges of the Jews and showing great insensitivity to the religious commitments of the people. For example, he ordered his troops to encamp in Jerusalem (the 'holy place'), and then sent them marching into the city with god-like images of the emperor attached to their ensigns. It was crude and offensive and hardly likely to endear him to Jewish believers.

Josephus's assessment of Pilate is paralleled in the New Testament. The Gospel writers point to his weakness and indecision, alongside his insensitivity. He is without creative imagination, which would have made his rule more flexible. He is intent on carrying out the formalities of Roman law, yet lacks the integrity and courage to ensure that justice is done. His fear of insurrection, and the effect this could have on his own career, seems to be his main preoccupation. If ever a man needed a wife with prophetic insight and clear conscience, it was clearly this one!

At the height of the tension, as Pilate is considering his verdict on the charges brought against Jesus, his wife breaks in on the story. Matthew includes her in a two-line narrative: 'While he was sitting on the judgement seat, his wife sent word to him. "Have nothing to do with that innocent man for today I have suffered a great deal because of a dream about him."' The message is brief but incredibly authoritative. The wife is giving her husband, the Roman governor, instructions on what he must and must not do. And this is not merely a domestic directive, akin to asking him if he will put the bins out; it is instruction in relation to his application of the weighty Roman law. His is the responsibility of legal judgement, but his wife takes this huge risk of interfering because she is afraid of the consequences of his doing the wrong thing. She has had a deep spiritual revelation in her dream, and its meaning to her is crystal clear. Jesus is innocent, a righteous man, and he must receive justice.

Her words clearly have an impact on her husband, but his own failings ultimately render him ineffective. Each of the Gospel writers says that Pilate finds no evidence against Jesus. Yet he fails to act decisively by ruling against the plaintiffs. Instead, he sends him to Herod, who affirms Pilate's conclusion and sends Jesus back. Finally, Pilate tries to bargain with the people, by giving them a choice of who to release. For him the choice is obvious. Barabbas is a convicted insurrectionist, a dangerous man. Jesus is a teacher who heals the sick. But Pilate is no match for the mob, who have been worked on by those who want Jesus to die. So, when his offer to release Jesus is turned down by the crowd and the religious leaders, Pilate has made himself impotent, and publicly washes his hands of the matter. In one sense he was doing what his wife had instructed. He was indeed having 'nothing to do with that righteous man'. Yet he was doing this not by respecting his wife's conviction and ensuring justice would be done but by abdicating all responsibility.

After this incident, we hear nothing further in the biblical text about Pilate's wife. We are left with our own reflections as to how she would have felt when she realized that she had failed to prevent the crucifixion. What must have been her thoughts when she saw Jesus struggling to carry his cross to the hill of Calvary where he would be nailed to it? It is more than likely that the turmoil she suffered would not have ended with Jesus' death, but that her husband's part in his execution would have remained with her for the rest of her life. All that history itself records through Josephus is that she stayed faithful to her husband and eventually went into exile with him. Pilate died in exile, probably committing suicide on the orders of the emperor.

What stands out from the story of her involvement is the faithfulness with which Pontius Pilate's wife acted on the revelation she had received. She didn't just sweep it away as inconsequential, or worry about what others might think of her. She knew that this was not simply a bad nightmare brought on by the wrong food before bed. Her dream had a divine source, identifying the righteousness of Jesus and impelling her to share the truth she had received. And she responded without hesitation or fear. Her experience was soon to be echoed in another revelation, received by the soldiers at the crucifixion when they called out, 'Truly, this man was the Son of God.'

Facing our challenges today

Pilate's wife did not realize it, but she was trying to change cosmic history. She wanted to prevent injustice, yet Christ was going to die in order to release salvation to the world. Nevertheless, Pilate remains accountable for his failure to do what was just, and her action remains vital in identifying the truth.

Few, if any, of us will be faced with issues of such cosmic significance, yet the story of Pilate's wife steers us in many ways. It reminds us that God can reach us through dreams. It is not only into our waking thoughts that God speaks, but occasionally our dreams themselves can give us a new awareness from God. Some dreams have helped women clarify a course of action in troublesome situations. Some have even led them into fresh revelations about the reality of God's self and about the relationship they can have with God. We have the testimony of Muslim women who have been prompted in dreams to look for the 'One who is called Father', which set them off on a new spiritual search and an encounter with Jesus.

Pilate's wife also teaches about the importance of speaking out. When faced with an issue of injustice, we are called to name it. Our world is full of injustice, where the vulnerable suffer and the voiceless go unheeded. When I researched my book on violence against women, I came across so many atrocities committed by people with power, whose victims went unnoticed and their oppression un-heeded. Yet it was so encouraging to discover that women of integrity were there too, breaking the silence and fight-ing the cause of others, often at cost to their own safety. This is a much-needed calling for all Christians, for with-out it injustice stands no chance of being eradicated.

Each year at Easter, the story of Pilate's wife reminds us that when we listen to God we hear the truth about Jesus. As she testified, he is indeed the righteous one, who com-mitted no wrong yet died for the sins of others. He is the one who calls his enemies to be his friends and prays for those who torture him. Her affirmation of his innocence remains true for every age. As we remember the story of his suffering and death, and her own plea for justice, we can teach his sacrificial love to our own culture and generation.

We can help those still without faith to understand the significance of Good Friday. We can affirm too that evil did not ultimately overcome him, but that powers of darkness were themselves defeated in the joy of his resurrection.

Questions to ponder

1 Try to imagine what it was like for Pilate's wife to confront her husband with the note about her dream. How would she have been feeling? What would have been the dominant anxieties?

2 What do you understand to be the key significance of the injustice meted out to Jesus? How does it fit into the biblical drama?

21

The women at the cross and tomb

**MATTHEW 27—28; MARK 15—16;
LUKE 23—24; JOHN 19—20**

The group of women who had travelled with Jesus on his journey from Galilee were still gathered at the cross in Jesus' final hour. For each one of them, it must have all felt like a nightmare. They had stood by, helpless, as the horrible events unfolded. Knowing Jesus so well, they could see that his last days on earth were marked with trauma and intense suffering. Who could cope with what they had to witness?

The physical ordeals Jesus went through must have distressed them terribly. He was flogged, worn out, made to drag a heavy cross up a hill, nailed through his hands and feet, hung for hours without support, deprived of water in intense heat and left to die in excruciating agony. The weight of his body finally crushed his lungs. Crucifixion was barbaric.

Yet the mental and emotion pain must also have been substantial. His male disciples had been ineffective, or worse. Judas was unstable and a thief, and betrayed him to his enemies. A group of others fell asleep when, in the garden of Gethsemane, he desperately needed them to pray. When he was arrested, they deserted him and ran. And Peter, who had been so close to Jesus, denied even knowing him. Despite their commitment to Jesus, the men were obviously petrified.

We can understand why. Their nation was under Roman occupation, which used the death penalty at will. Jesus' followers knew how extreme state violence could be. Two thousand revolutionaries had been tortured and crucified during their own childhood. The cross was the biggest Roman fear-machine. It demonstrated the power and domination of that great empire, controlling dissidents and dissuading insurrection. It symbolized the authority of the Roman Empire over life and death, reflecting the military force and might of a world power that could crush all that stood against it. Fear of crucifixion would make anyone think twice about raising their voice or showing disobedience to the emperor. We should not be surprised, then, that the disciples chose to keep a low profile.

What is perhaps more surprising is that the women disciples didn't. They were not afraid of being known as the Nazarene's friends. The Gospel writers remind us that the group included Mary Magdalene, Salome, the wife of Zebedee, Mary, Joanna, his own mother and the mother of James and Joseph. They stayed as close to the cross of Jesus as they could during the long hours of his agonizing death. They wept, heartbroken, as they saw him struggle with pain. They listened in grief as he asked his disciple John to care for his mother. They could not even leave when the body was taken down from the cross, but instead followed

Joseph of Arimathea to see where his corpse would be laid. The women who had supported Jesus throughout his ministry and received so many blessings from him were not going to disown him now. They were determined to pay their last respects and anoint his body.

Women, of course, had a special role in rituals of death. Even in normal circumstances, they would clean and embalm the body and lead the procession of mourners. And the women here were fully committed to caring for the body of the one they loved. But these were not normal circumstances. Everything was complicated. To start with, the Roman execution had to be finished before the Jewish Sabbath began, to ensure some semblance of civic peace. The rush to get the bodies away meant that the soldiers had to break the legs of the breathing men crucified with Jesus, to bring on their death. The body of Jesus was dispatched with the same haste before night fell. The Sabbath meant that the women must wait. They could gather and prepare their spices, but they couldn't embalm Jesus' body until some 36 hours after his death.

Those hours must have been terrible. We can imagine the torment of waiting together, longing for the hours to pass as they needed to see their dear friend's body. Other problems would confront them too. Guards had been posted at the burial place. What if they refused access to the women? And the huge stone that covered the entrance to the tomb – who would roll it away for them?

These challenges faced the women as they waited to go to the tomb. Were they afraid? Or were they empowered by their desire to pour love on the broken body of their dear friend and teacher? We don't know. I would imagine that there was little chatter as they walked towards the place of burial. It was the third day, and barely dawn. We do know they thought they were prepared for the difficulties they might encounter. Yet we also know that they were utterly unprepared for what confronted them when they arrived. We can imagine their amazement when they found the stone already rolled away, the linen cloths lying there, but no body.

The Gospel writers offer slightly different accounts of the women's visit to the tomb. After all, four people are each telling the story, and their narratives are authentic. Matthew, Mark and Luke mention that all the women came to the tomb; John mentions only Mary Magdalene. Two of the writers describe the encounter between the women and an angel. Luke's account gives two angels, while John focuses on Mary's confusion, and the angels appear later. Yet every one of the writers affirms that the stone was rolled away, the tomb was open and there was no corpse. Each writer describes how the women are assured that Jesus has risen from the dead. And all the Gospels tell us that, rather than embalming a body, the women are sent back to give out the good news of resurrection. The male disciples, predictably, can barely believe what the women tell them.

We know the story of the resurrection so well that we don't always realize the incredible significance given to the women. Their role runs counter to all the limitations women faced in that society. Women could certainly fulfil domestic tasks, but they held a subordinate-place role, legally, economically and religiously. In the Temple, women were not allowed to worship alongside the men, or go beyond the women's court. In a court of law, a woman's testimony was usually disregarded if it was not corroborated by a man or several other witnesses. Yet, despite their lack of legal credibility, God chose women as the first ones to testify to Christ's resurrection. Despite their low religious status, they were the ones God sent to impart the good news that death had been swallowed up in victory. God's choice of women as ambassadors to Christ's victory turned their cultural status on its head and reinforced the value that God placed on them. The women accepted their calling. Once the angels had reminded them of Jesus' promise, they realized that they had been given the most crucial message in the world. With hope in God completely restored, they set out with confidence to proclaim that Christ was risen from the dead. That proclamation has resounded through history, and is ours today.

Facing our challenges today

The story is encouraging for women, whatever culture we are in. Its headline statement is that in God's creation and redemption women are significant. God has made us to reflect his love for others. He calls us and equips us to be his envoys. He entrusts us with communicating the good news of Christ. God bestows us with dignity, whatever our circumstances. The women who stayed by Jesus knew the truth of this. They could not fight their social status, but they worked with it. They were less of a political threat to the authorities than men, who could potentially become a fighting force. So the women took advantage of their subordinate standing and worked with it. Despite the patriarchal context of their lives, God used them to bring liberating change.

Today, in societies that are still heavily patriarchal, Christian women can find they have freedom when they work together. Women have been able to protect children from being trafficked, smuggle Bibles into prohibited areas, and preach Christ's love when forbidden by the authorities. In the Congo, I came across groups of women who unobtrusively patrolled the streets, safeguarding girls against rape and sexual assault; in China, Christian women worked with others trapped in prostitution, quietly sharing the gospel and helping them to find a way out. Following Christ always opens us to risk, but, like the women at the tomb, women today face those risks with courage.

A different challenge that confronted these women is very much present for Christian women in secularized societies. That is, to keep faith alive. For the women waiting to embalm the body, it must have felt that all hope had gone. They had trusted Jesus and now he was dead. Life seemed pointless. And as our own cultures move ever further away from the Christian faith, into entrenched materialism and unbelief, Christian women might have to deal with levels of doubt and scepticism that can rock their faith and leave them too feeling life is pointless. Especially at times of emotional fragility and loss, this challenge can be overwhelming. It is isolating too. With spiritual faith banished from our nation's daily agenda of individual self-interest and consumerism, many of us might long to have a visit from angels to reassure us that God is real.

That is why we need to be constant in prayer for those who are going through turmoil or struggling with fear. Our prayer reconnects them with the faith of millions throughout the world. We need to pray for ourselves too, as Jesus told his disciples at Gethsemane. For we all need protection from evil, and courage for the journey ahead. Prayer is where God meets us in the power of the Holy Spirit. Prayer is where we can have encounters with angels and know guidance for the future. Despite the forces of darkness that press in, each one of us can find our hope renewed, our faith rekindled, our purpose restored. For Christ's resurrection power was not just for those sorrowing women in that culture over two thousand years ago. People across the whole world in every age can know power and truth because Christ is risen. And we too can echo that truth: 'He is risen indeed!'

Questions to ponder

1 What strikes you most in the four Gospel accounts of the women at the cross and tomb – their differences or similarities? What are the benefits of having four accounts with different nuances, rather than one single account repeated?
2 What difference does Christ's resurrection make to your own life?

22

Mary of Magdala: apostle to the apostles

LUKE 8.1–3; JOHN 20.14–17

All four Gospels include Mary Magdalene in their accounts of those who visited the tomb. The Gospel of John gives a very full account of her encounter with the risen Christ. A flurry of interest has been shown regarding this woman beyond the Church. For she excites the imagination of many secular writers and film-makers, all of whom are keen to find new angles on the biblical narrative. So who was Mary Magdalene, and what was her history?

Mary was a Jewish woman from the fishing town of Magdala, which lay on the western shore of the Sea of Galilee. We know nothing of her family background, or childhood, but we do know that when she met Jesus she was a very troubled woman. As we noted earlier, she is mentioned first in the Gospels of Mark and Luke, in the context of the group of women close to Jesus. Like Joanna, she had been healed by him. In Mary's case it was through a form of exorcism, for Jesus had cast out 'seven demons' from her. Numbers are not always meant literally in the New Testament, and 'seven' is a number often associated with totality. It is quite likely that she was suffering from a condition of multiple personalities where many different 'parts' were struggling for dominance in her life. Her condition was very serious and she may indeed have been living a life of near total bondage to her demons.

The severe emotional and psychological trauma that Mary must have been suffering required Jesus to heal her in this special way. Far more often, Jesus healed people without exorcism, even when their condition might otherwise call for it. Neither Luke nor Mark dwells on the details of Mary's disorder. But if it was anything like the disorder exhibited by another person subject to 'multiple demons' in the Gospels, it would have been dramatic. The condition of 'Legion', the 'possessed man', had left him battered and bruised, without dignity or control, before the exorcism. As far as the bystanders were concerned, he was deranged. To most onlookers, Mary too would have seemed anguished and beyond their help, and thus to be avoided. But when Jesus looked at her he saw the real Mary and restored her.

We don't know how the exorcism was performed, whether the complete change was instant or whether full healing took place over some time. We are simply told that Jesus had commanded the demons to depart and, at the time of the story, she was well. Nothing more is recorded about her sickness. They wanted us to know she had moved on; her healing had enabled her to reassert her true identity and live free from what had tortured her. They regarded her as an important member of the group of faithful women followers who supported Jesus and enjoyed his teaching.

It is John's account of the resurrection, however, that gives us the deepest understanding of Mary. John takes us through in detail how she faces the challenge of fear and unbelief. Going to the tomb early in the morning, her task is to embalm Jesus' body, and her worry is that they will not be able to move the stone and gain entrance. Instead, when she finds the stone has been rolled away, she jumps immediately to the conclusion that the body has been removed. We can understand the shock. This was not expected. Her assumption was perfectly normal. From where she stood in the entrance, the tomb would have looked alarmingly empty.

Her first impulse is to go back to tell the other disciples and share her distress at not knowing where Jesus' body is now. Peter and John come back immediately with her to see for themselves. Peter, direct as ever, rushes straight into the tomb to view a pile of empty linen strips and the cloth that had covered the face. All he witnesses confirms Mary's fear. The body has been taken away. While they go back to tell the others, Mary stays there, weeping and utterly confused. She seems rooted to the place where Jesus ought to have been. She has no idea what has happened to the body. She can't pay her last loving respects to the one who means everything to her. But where else is there to go? It must have seemed that her mental and emotional world was collapsing again. As if she had not been overwhelmed enough by the awful execution, and the torture of seeing Jesus die, now she has to face the theft of his body. The authorities were leaving them nothing to hold on to, not even a body to care for in death.

For many of us, faith often comes through tears. It does for Mary. As she weeps and picks up the courage to enter the tomb, she is slowly given a different picture. In the death-gloom of the sepulchre, angelic light appears where Jesus' body had been lying. She speaks to the angels, asking them where the body has gone. They don't answer. She becomes aware of a man behind her and thinks he's the gardener, so asks him the same question. It is only when Jesus utters her name that she recognizes him and begins to be aware of a whole new reality. Unbelievable joy suddenly floods her. There is no body because Jesus is alive. And here he is. Her instincts are to run and embrace him, but Jesus restrains her. We don't know why he doesn't want physical contact, except that his risen body has its own tasks now to accomplish. He sends her instead to the other disciples, with the incredible message of his resurrection and coming ascension. Jesus commissions Mary as the apostle to the apostles.

The Mary that John presents in this moving narrative is a woman of love and trust, but one who also lives in a world where cause and effect explains events. If a tomb stone has been moved, and the tomb is missing a corpse once placed there, the only reasonable explanation can be that the body has been forcibly taken away. The challenge for Mary is to go on believing, trusting God, in spite of the evidence of her senses and the reasoning of her mind. Yet this challenge does not last long, for Jesus himself confirms the true reality and gives her the evidence that she will always remember. Mary's testimony acknowledges that there is more to reality than materialist explanations, for she has seen the risen Lord. And this echoes across centuries and brings people of all nations to faith.

Facing our challenges today

Many of us might wish we could see Jesus for ourselves and have our faith affirmed. Today, as in Mary's day, we still contend with unbelief, doubt and fear. Some do see Jesus in visions or dreams. Some people see angels, and are so convinced by them that issues they were struggling with are resolved and overcome. But we also remember Jesus' own words after his resurrection, to Thomas: 'Because you have seen me, you have believed; blessed are those who have not seen and yet have believed.'

Jesus recognized that it would make a difference to his followers that he was no longer present physically in the world. So he gives us another Presence, that of the Holy Spirit. The Spirit is also spoken of in personal terms, though not in gendered terms, and is not merely a force or a feeling or an idea, but is a comforter, rebuker, counsellor, advocate. The Holy Spirit gives us discernment, wisdom, fruit, gifts, and is the Spirit of truth, who challenges us to seek the mind of Christ and reject the lies that worm their way into relationships, nations, economics, values. We face all our challenges in life with the Spirit's help.

We need to realize that when Jesus comes to us through the Holy Spirit, he comes primarily to us together, as his body, the Church. Individual believers have spiritual gifts; they might be prophets or have words of discernment. But authority is not vested in them. The Holy Spirit is to be discerned by the whole body of Christ, and we are to wait on God's leading and empowering. What is more, the Holy Spirit never leads us into anything that contradicts the teaching of Jesus, never colluding with corruption, greed, autocratic control, hatred, racism or misogyny. Far too many people have claimed to be speaking for the Holy Spirit when they have been pushing their own ideas and agendas.

Mary teaches us something very significant in this respect. It is the importance of humility. Mary came to the tomb not to prove anything but simply to offer Jesus her final, humble act of love – the anointing of his cold, dead body. Instead, she found the presence of angels and a risen Saviour. She was convinced by a single word – her own name – and went out in faith and love to share her experiences with the other believers. Her motivation was not to defend what she believed but just to honour Jesus. Each step she took was not about herself but about Jesus. Her response to the other apostles was not to assert her superiority in being the first to see Jesus alive, but to share with them the risen Christ. Mary is not simply the apostle to the apostles, but an apostle to us also.

Mary's example reminds us that we are inevitably at risk of getting things wrong, because, as humans, we are never free from the effects of sin and error. Yet humility in the body of Christ enables us to discern the Spirit's leading. Listening to one another, and praying together in the body of Christ, guards against false claims and focuses us more on Jesus. Christ is as alive today as he was when Mary met him outside the tomb and supposed him to be the gardener. And God's love in Christ will always be in evidence when those who believe on his name worship him in humility and love.

Questions to ponder

1 Why do you think that Mary of Magdala has excited so much interest and attention from secular people in our culture? What is it about Mary that draws your own interest?

2 Mary recognized Jesus when he spoke her name. Do you ever have the sense that God knows your name and is aware of your concerns? How would you describe that?

23

Lydia: taking a risk with her hospitality

ACTS 16.9–15

So far, the focus in this book has been on the women in the Hebrew Scriptures and the Gospels. But the story of women in a patriarchal world continues after the death and resurrection of Jesus. Jesus had offered a different vision, which challenged patriarchy and reaffirmed women in their value and significance. Yet the surrounding culture was slow to change. The task now fell to the followers of Christ to implement that vision and challenge the prevailing culture. How well they accomplished this task is still a matter of debate.

Although his references to women are quite often misunderstood, St Paul was instrumental in challenging the old ways of seeing things. He found it normal to work in partnership with women in the task of evangelism. We are told that on his second missionary journey St Paul had a vision. A vision of Jesus had first stopped him from persecuting Christians and led him to be a follower. Now, in this other vision, a man has pleaded with him to 'come over to Macedonia' to help them. This was quite a request, as Paul was a long way from Macedonia. He could have been forgiven if he had put this manifestation down to indigestion! But he had no doubt that this was from God. So he gathered his team and they quickly set off across the Aegean Sea towards what is now the northern region of modern-day Greece. Once there, they headed straight for Philippi, a key city and Roman colony. What they found, however, must have come as a surprise. There was no man in a synagogue with others, waiting for Paul to help them, but a group of women gathered in a prayer place near the river. One of these women was Lydia. Before she had even met Paul, she was already a spiritual searcher committed to knowing God more.

The Acts of the Apostles is a book packed with accounts of people who meet Paul and his team on their missionary journeys. Luke likes to document these encounters, but usually gives us only scant descriptions of the people themselves: 'a slave girl', 'the jailor', 'a crippled man', 'a magistrate of the city', 'some philosophers'. The gospel had an impact on many people, and Luke would have found it difficult to record all their names and backgrounds. Yet Luke provides a good deal of information about Lydia. He tells us she came from the city of Thyatira (in the western part of the Roman province of Asia – Turkey, today). Thyatira was a prosperous commercial hub, located at the junction of major trade routes and noted for its guilds. Many people worked in textiles, manufacturing and dyeing fabrics. One particular dye, purple, was derived from marine molluscs and particularly expensive. It was used in luxury items, highly sought after by the wealthy elite. So when Luke tells us Lydia was a seller of purple cloth and from Thyatira, we're clearly meant to understand she had some significance in the public sphere of the first-century Roman world. By the time Luke and Paul met her, she was a relatively prosperous purple-cloth trader, settled comfortably in Philippi and with a large household.

Luke also lets us know that Lydia was a spiritual seeker. She met the other women by the river, because they could not meet in the city. Inscribed on arches outside Philippi was a prohibition against bringing any 'unrecognized' (that is, non-pagan) religion within. So the prayer house seems to have been a place where Jewish women would gather to encourage each other and pray, though there could well have been women there who came out of paganism and cultic worship. Whoever was there, Luke singles out Lydia among the women in the prayer house as 'a worshipper of God'. She was already one of the leaders of the group, skilled in networking and relating to others. And when the Christian missionaries arrived there, they found the women receptive and ready to hear their teaching. Lydia, in particular, listened eagerly to Paul's message as 'God opened her heart' to receive the truth about Jesus.

Lydia's response was immediate. Not only did she accept the good news of the gospel and believe, she also accepted the need to make her new commitment to Christ public. She and her household were baptized. We don't know how many others of that women's prayer group joined them as the missionaries took them into baptism, probably in the nearby river. But it was certainly a time of rejoicing, for both the new converts and the missionaries, and, in fact, an immediate fulfilment of Paul's vision.

Luke records that Lydia invited them all to stay at her home, as confirmation that she was now truly one of them – 'a believer in the Lord'. And they went, gladly accepting her warm and generous hospitality. This part of the story is curious. She did not go to ask permission of a husband or male relative. In fact, there is no mention in the story of any man on whom Lydia was dependent, or to whom she was subject. She may have been widowed or never married. It is clear, however, that she was her own mistress; the house was hers and she could invite anyone she wished. The house must also have been spacious – large enough to accommodate Paul, Timothy, Silas, Luke and whoever else was in the visiting party, as well as her own household. The hospitality would have been costly; a huge amount of food to be provided, as well as servants to do the work.

A greater cost, however, was in the risk to safety involved. Like most cities under Roman occupation, Philippi was home to idol worship. Hosting a group of foreign men who preached a Jewish Messiah could well ruin Lydia's professional reputation. And Roman gods and goddesses were more than lumps of marble. They also stood for civic pride and money. The silversmiths and goldsmiths made a fortune from domestic images of idols, and the temples collected revenue from worshippers. Lydia would have known that any religion that touched their profits would be strongly opposed. In Ephesus, the preaching of the gospel had brought a near riot as silversmiths urged protestors to take to the streets shouting, 'Great is Diana of the Ephesians!' So her new Christian faith brought Lydia a big challenge. Just how big became evident when Paul and Silas cast a spirit out of a fortune-telling slave with demonic prophetic powers, to the fury of her masters. The missionaries were seized, convicted, flogged and jailed. Lydia's whole household could well have been put under threat.

The story unfolded in a totally unexpected way, however. First, God organized an earthquake, which shook the prison and freed Paul and Silas. Terrified that his prisoners had escaped, the jailor was about to commit suicide, but Paul stopped him and shared the gospel instead. Immediately becoming a Christian, he washed their wounds and offered his own hospitality to the pair. The next day, when the authorities told Paul and Silas they were free to go, they refused. They pointed out they were Roman citizens and by being flogged and imprisoned without trial they had been treated unlawfully. The arrogance of the authorities immediately crumbled. We can well imagine the fear that must have gripped them. In the end, they provided Paul and Silas with an escort to return to Lydia's house, all threats now removed.

Lydia's own boldness in standing by the missionaries bore wonderful fruit. Her home became the meeting place for the growing Christian movement in Philippi, and she was most likely one of the leaders of the early church there. Paul gives his final exhortation in her house before leaving. It is clear that without Lydia's partnership and resources Paul's preaching and evangelism might never have produced a flourishing Christian community in the city or contested the idols of their age.

Facing our challenges today

The thing we learn most of all from Lydia is the priority we need to give to our calling as Christians. Once she had taken the step of faith and embraced the gospel, Lydia's priorities changed. She did not stop being a business-woman but her life was now centred on being a *believing* business woman. Now she traded in purple cloth in order to exercise Christian hospitality and help the church grow. Her home, her resources and her energy were given to God for whatever purpose they were needed. This reordering of our lives is crucial for women today. If we are to be effective Christians in our time, the same integration of faith and life is asked of us too. Our calling as Christians may involve our giving up what we were doing before, starting a whole new journey, maybe training for a new profession, champi-oning causes or going overseas. Or it may mean that we continue as before, but with new purpose and meaning as we integrate our work with a biblical world and life view.

We might also face a level of persecution in our culture for what we believe. There are those, even in our society, who would stop Christians from praying with others, or speak-ing out on moral issues. Increasingly, there are restrictions on preaching in public places. Standing by convictions can be costly for any of us, and can present a challenge whatever our walk of life. We only find out what this means for our own discipleship through prayer and seeking God.

Finally, Lydia challenges us to face our own signifi-cance in the spread of the gospel. Women were not at the margins in the early Christian Church; neither silent in churches nor absent in evangelism. They were effective communicators and vital in the expansion of mission. The church in Philippi owes its existence to the Holy Spirit's work through Paul's preaching and Lydia's open heart and open home. In the same way, women's ministries of teaching and hospitality are vital today. God uses us powerfully, across the world, in the growth of the gospel and the nurture of faith.

Questions to ponder

1 Lydia's enthusiasm was matched by her energy, and they provided the backcloth for many of the opportunities that Paul had in Thyatira. When you look at your own church, to what extent does enthusiasm and energy forge local opportunities?

2 Dreams and visions play a significant part in God's communication with people in the Bible. Modern psychology might question whether some of this is wishful thinking. What stories have you heard that sound authentic?

24

Priscilla teaches Apollos some theology

ACTS 18.1–3, 18–28

I would love to have met Priscilla. She seems to have been the sort of perceptive and engaging Christian woman we all need in our lives. She was certainly very significant in the early Church, as we learn from both the Acts of the Apostles and the letters of St Paul. Her name is mentioned at least six times in the New Testament, along with that of her husband Aquila.

We don't have much early biographical detail of Priscilla (or Prisca, as she's also called), but that is not unusual in the New Testament. We don't know where she first heard the gospel or when she became a follower of Jesus. It is likely that she was a Gentile and may have come from Pontus, like her Jewish husband. We pick up her story when she was already in her adulthood. According to Acts 18, Priscilla and Aquila had been among the Jews expelled from Rome by the Roman emperor Claudius. The historian Suetonius put the date for that at AD 49, but the reasons for the mass expulsion are not clear. It could have been because the growth of Christianity among the Jewish population was causing unrest, or because Claudius simply didn't want

Jews around. Either way, the couple fled from Italy and by AD 51 had settled in Corinth.

It is clear from all the references to them in the New Testament that they were missionaries and apologists, engaging with local people and arguing for the faith. In Corinth, they worked as tent-makers, which is why St Paul first joined them – it was his trade also. It is interesting that 'tent-making' is the title given even today to Christian outreach workers who are self-financing. Priscilla and Aquila knew the trade literally, earning their living with their hands as they made and repaired tents. It was a significant job. Tents were dwelling places where people might live for whole periods of their lives. Often they were made of leather and required considerable crafting skill in their manufacture. So this married couple, along with their colleague Paul, resourced people both practically and spiritually as they constructed their tents and preached the gospel.

We can picture the routines of the day that would shape the next 18 months, the three evangelists working away methodically at their manual trade, while sharing their knowledge of the Hebrew Scriptures. They must have spent hours discussing with others the unique significance of Jesus as the one who had been foretold by the prophets. During those months they became convinced through many incidents that they were being called to evangelize and church-plant not only in Corinth but in Ephesus and Rome as well. So preparations got underway. By the spring of AD 52, Paul, Priscilla and Aquila were ready to set sail. They headed towards Caesarea (now Syria) but stopped at Ephesus, where Paul left Priscilla and Aquila. They stayed behind to spread the gospel while he continued on. When Paul returned to Ephesus about a year later (during his third missionary journey), he was thrilled to discover that the couple had established a Christian congregation in their house (1 Corinthians 16.19). By then, they were well established in their leadership and highly respected among both the apostles and Christian converts. Paul referred to them, warmly, as his 'co-workers in Christ Jesus' (Romans 16.3).

Paul's enthusiasm towards them is not unusual. He often spoke affectionately of people who laboured with him in the gospel. Yet one thing is unusual. In his five references to the couple, four times Paul mentions Priscilla's name first. This is not simply to observe protocol. In fact, it's a departure from what would have been protocol, as the higher status of the man would have been acknowledged by his being mentioned first. So why did Paul make this inversion? Most New Testament scholars agree that it signifies that Priscilla had a more public ministry than her husband and was a widely accepted Christian leader.

Priscilla's position did bring its own challenges. She still lived in a patriarchal society where the authority of men was deemed more important and where women were expected to accept that authority without question. In one encounter, those expectations must have left her with a considerable dilemma.

Another evangelist had come to Ephesus and was gaining the ear of the people. He was the brilliant and eloquent Apollos, a native of Alexandria, and very enthusiastic in his faith. He was also learned in the Hebrew Scriptures and bold in his teaching in the synagogue that Jesus was the

Messiah. Yet Priscilla was also disturbed by his teaching. The text tells us that he 'only knew the baptism of John'. In other words, he knew the need for repentance but had not yet developed the full message of Christ's atonement and the empowering of the Holy Spirit. So the couple faced a serious issue. How could they help Apollos preach the gospel more fully?

I find it interesting that they did not see Apollos as a rival, or show any jealousy towards his success in preaching. They were not arrogant or dismissive of his teaching. They respected his learning and zeal. But they simply wanted him to bring greater honour to Jesus, and open up the full meaning of Christ's salvation for others. So they befriended him, engaged with him and gently shared their own insights. The result was that Apollos fully accepted their teaching and became a pioneer evangelist and leading figure in the early Church. The early Christian writer John Chrysostom (c. 349–407) sees the contribution of Priscilla as utterly vital in this process: 'She took Apollos, an eloquent man and powerful in the scriptures, but knowing only the baptism of John; and she instructed him in the way of the Lord and made him a teacher brought to completion' (John Chrysostom, *First Homily on the Greeting to Priscilla and Aquila*, J. P. Migne, *Patrologia Graeca* 51.187 (1857–66), trans. Catherine Kroeger, 1989). It's clear from the biblical text that neither Paul nor Luke saw it as inappropriate for Priscilla to correct publicly the teachings of a man. They did not hide her effectiveness in public office. This calls for those who maintain that Paul discouraged all women from teaching to revise their assumptions. For

Priscilla's actions were accepted without question and her leadership was definitively endorsed by the New Testament writers.

Facing our challenges today

Priscilla's example is of great help to those women called to a public Christian ministry. She sets the bar high, but shows it is also achievable. Four key characteristics stand out for me. First, she was a team player, not simply a solo artist. And although her team was packed with leading men in the early Church, she was a significant contributor. The apostle Paul, her own husband Aquila, doctor Luke, the dynamic evangelist Apollos, and probably Timothy also, were enriched by her companionship and leadership. Women have been missionary leaders throughout history and today take crucial leadership roles in team ministries right across the world. God continues to call us.

Second, Priscilla's motivations were gospel-directed, and her attitudes were gracious and generous. Women leading congregations or undertaking outreach and evangelism need to keep their minds focused on the centrality of their calling and not be deflected by envy, pride or jealousy. This is not always easy, especially when they see men far less talented than themselves being pivoted into key positions while they are offered more mundane opportunities. Yet in many communities the women who have the authenticity of a Jesus-directed life still emerge as the 'real leaders'. Others grow through their ministry and are empowered. When our motivation is simply to bring honour to God and help people to follow Jesus, our leadership too will speak through whatever other structures are in place.

Third, Priscilla was willing to apply herself to learning the Hebrew Scriptures so that she supported her evangelism with real knowledge and not simply her own opinions. This is vital for those of us today who feel called to lead others. It's too easy to promote our own views and claim that they are the work of the Holy Spirit, rather than immerse ourselves in the Scriptures and sometimes be self-critical. But we need to understand our faith correctly. And this priority takes time – a lifetime in fact. Yet without this we will quickly be out of our depth before the issues that confront us today. Christian knowledge and wisdom remain the bedrock of the Church.

Finally, Priscilla was not cowed by the patriarchal systems of her day. It must have taken some courage and confidence to approach someone of Apollos's learning and correct him, but she did it nevertheless. Women leaders in our time might need the courage to take on people with big names whose theology is dubitable. We might even have to engage with cultural opinion-formers, those who develop secular orthodoxies and those who deny the faith. Priscilla's commitment to the truth encourages us. We can find that, empowered by the Holy Spirit, we can do this also; we might even find it's a crucial part of our calling as women today.

Questions to ponder

1 Why is it important that Priscilla was a tent-maker, and what does it say about the 'sacred–secular' division that some people seem to create?

2 The spiritual authority that God vested in Priscilla made it easier for Paul to see her as a co-worker in the gospel. How do we detect authentic spiritual authority in church leadership today?

25

Euodia and Syntyche go down in history

PHILIPPIANS 4.1–3

Not all the women who faced challenges in the Bible are our role models; some are negative examples of Christian discipleship. Yet they still have much to teach us. This is so true of the last two women leaders we meet in this book, whose names come up in relation to the church at Philippi.

Euodia and Syntyche were not missionaries like Priscilla, nor church-planters like Lydia. But they were in active leadership in the growing church at Philippi, demonstrating again the gender-inclusive calling of Christ. And their story reminds us that even in the early Church, when people were much closer than they are today to the life and times of Jesus, problems could flare up that seriously hindered the work of the gospel.

St Paul mentions Euodia and Syntyche in his letter to the church at Philippi. He singles out a number of individuals in that letter, so this reference is not unusual. Yet the nature of the reference is unusual, and Paul leaves us with more questions than answers. The women are in some kind of dispute with each other; it sounds serious and Paul calls on the whole church to help them heal the breach. But what is the issue? Paul is tantalizingly reticent to identify the source of the problem, and generations of Bible readers have had to decide for themselves what the dispute was about. Alas, we can't fill in the gaps, as the details are lost in the mists of time. But we can begin to understand why the challenge faced by Euodia and Syntyche was significant for the whole fellowship. Let's start by recalling what was happening in the early Church.

Paul had been sent by the apostles to take the good news overseas. His powerful conversion and experience of the Holy Spirit had changed him from someone trying to serve God through killing to someone preaching the love of Christ. The apostles themselves remained mostly in Jerusalem, while Paul and his missionary companions (including Priscilla and Aquila) travelled around the Mediterranean region and into Asia Minor. Initially, this would have been no great upheaval for Paul, for he was born in Tarsus (in what is now Turkey), and travel had been part of his early life. Even though he was part of a strict Jewish family, he would have been more familiar with the cities of Derbe and Lystra than with Jerusalem. From a human point of view, he was also a cosmopolitan, educated, informed Roman citizen who spoke Greek and other languages.

Nevertheless, to travel to Western cities, like Philippi or Rome, would have been quite a challenge, as they involved long journeys across both land and sea, and a good deal of cultural adjustment. From the letters that Paul wrote to the small new Christian communities, we can sense that the task of evangelism and church-planting brought him great encouragement but also considerable issues to work through.

The church at Philippi had begun partly through that group of women who met with Lydia for prayer (Acts 16.11–15), as we saw earlier. Lydia's networking and hospitality had provided an important base and the church had grown. Euodia and Syntyche may well have been in the original group at prayer with Lydia, but even if they weren't they were certainly very involved in the Philippian church by now. They would have been well tutored by Paul and Silas, and committed to living out their faith.

The two women had thrown themselves wholeheartedly into the work of the gospel. Paul acknowledges this warmly in his letters and assures his readers that the names of these women are written in the 'book of life' – a reference to their salvation in Christ. Interestingly, he also calls them 'co-workers', a term used only for those with some public ministry or leadership in the church. Paul uses the same term, elsewhere, to describe Apollos (1 Corinthians 3.9), Prisca and Aquila (Romans 16.3–4), Silas (1 Thessalonians 3.2), Timothy (Romans 16.21) and Titus (2 Corinthians 8.23).

John Chrysostom, the early church theologian, points out that Paul commends the two women in exactly the same way as he commends his male co-workers and companions. Paul's own description of the women 'struggling' alongside him in the work of the gospel conveys that their calling has not been without cost or sacrifice. Chrysostom is quite sure that Euodia and Syntyche were significant leaders in the church at Philippi, and in one of his homilies he compares them to Phoebe, a leader in the church at Cenchrea.

Yet praise for the two women is, sadly, only half the story. Paul singles them out in his letter not to commend them for their work but to ask them to get on with each other. They seem to have been embroiled in a prolonged quarrel, which has now become detrimental to the work and witness to Jesus. His words are emphatic. 'I plead with Euodia and I plead with Syntyche to be of the same mind in the Lord. Yes, and I ask you, my true companion, help these women.'

So, what was the argument about? Many writers have entertained us with various suggestions, but the truth is that we just don't know. It is unlikely to have been a fundamental clash of personality, since the women had clearly worked well together in the past. Maybe it was about procedures: who should do what, how they should divide the mentoring; small differences can easily lead to major disputes. Or there could have been personal issues, some jealousy perhaps, or judgemental words spoken in haste, or even family disputes. There's no end of possibilities. The only thing we do know is that these two women were at odds with each other.

Paul's deepest concern was to pass on the vision he had received from Christ: Christians should not conform to the values and morals predominant in the cultures they lived in, but be transformed by the Holy Spirit, to establish a new, faithful and loving way of life. Christ's followers were not to be driven by self-righteousness or self-interest, but were to look out for the needs of others. They were not to operate on status or superiority, but were to see one another as vital parts of the body of Christ. They were not to be quarrelsome or contentious but to work effectively together in mutual care and concern. Christians were, above all, to allow the mind of Christ to dwell in the Church and demonstrate the compassion and grace of God for all to see.

The dispute between Euodia and Syntyche clearly undermined this. And by the time of Paul's letter, the row had reached crisis point. It was so public across the growing churches that Paul heard about it even while he was chained up in a Roman prison! And the implications were worrying. Two women in public contention could easily have drawn other people into factions around them, putting the unity of the whole group of believers in Philippi in jeopardy. So Paul names the disagreement and calls upon them all to resolve it. Paul's insistence was that Christians needed to emulate Jesus' own attitudes and outlook. For, even though he was equal with God, Jesus never focused on his status or sought his own way. Instead, he 'emptied himself' and became a servant to other people. To have the 'mind of Christ', the two women should have been showing each other respect and caring for the needs of others.

Euodia and Syntyche were not the only people to know discord in the early Church. Paul himself had parted company with Barnabas because they could not agree on a travelling companion. Yet they both moved on with God and the Church flourished. It would be good to know how the women faced the challenge of putting their differences aside. Were they able to repent, forgive one another and be reconciled? Again, we don't know. We never got an update on the issue from Paul. But we do know that the church in Philippi continued to grow, so it is more than possible that, with the encouragement of the whole church, the dispute was resolved. Sadly, however, this would not be the last time that followers of Christ would be unable to get on with each other.

Facing our challenges today

Being able to get on with sisters and fellow believers is still one of the most common challenges facing the Church. It's easier when we're with people like ourselves, sharing a similar temperament or outlook. But churches are not simply for the like-minded. The gospel draws in people from so many different ages, outlooks and backgrounds. We shouldn't expect always to see eye to eye. Our calling is not to construct an identikit Christian group but to demonstrate unity in diversity.

Having the 'mind of Christ' has huge implications for relationships. It means we shouldn't stand in judgement on one another, or gossip about someone, or put another Christian down. Nor should we flatter other people in order to be liked by them. A worst-case scenario is when we heap praise and affirmation on someone, while quietly resenting them or speaking ill of them to someone else. Tragically, these attitudes are found as much in the Church as anywhere, but they are foreign to a gospel way of living.

Euodia and Syntyche had their hands full in working to spread the gospel. The good news of Christ's atoning death and the victory of his resurrection had to reach beyond the Church, to draw people into faith. But resentment, bad relationships and quarrels send the wrong message. The challenge, instead, is to build up good relationships, where we can be open with each other, trusting enough to share confidences and speak the truth in love. Thankfully, right through the centuries, so many women have been able to do this and be involved in mutually enriching Christian work. The positive results have been seen in the outworking of hospitality, teaching, organizing, nurturing, evangelizing, preaching, networking and counselling. Today, this work goes on.

At the heart of a good relationship is mutual humility, being ready to serve the other and pray God's blessing on the other with complete sincerity. It involves being ready to forgive when we're offended and apologize when we're in the wrong. Paul wanted this for the church at Philippi; God wants it for our churches today. When we have no ego to defend, and no self to justify, the process of reconciliation is so much easier to achieve. In no period in history has the Church ever got things completely right. In no church on earth are relationships completely sorted. For until time itself ends, all our work before God is unfinished business and we, as church, are a work in progress. Yet God's Spirit does empower us to live out the gospel in our lives with each other, whoever and wherever we are. And through us that same Spirit can make God's love in Christ evident across the world and transform hearts and lives today.

Questions to ponder

1 What do you see in Paul's letter that helped the Philippian church to grow, despite the wrangle between two of its leaders?

2 How important is the ministry of reconciliation in your own church? Is it something you can offer to those in conflict outside?

An easy way to get to know the Bible

'For those who've been putting aside two years in later life to read the Bible from cover to cover, the good news is: the most important bits are here.' Jeremy Vine, BBC Radio 2

The Bible is full of dramatic stories that have made it the world's bestselling book. But whoever has time to read it all from cover to cover? Now here's a way of getting to know the Bible without having to read every chapter and verse.

No summary, no paraphrase, no commentary: just the Bible's own story in the Bible's own words.

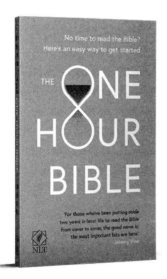

'What an amazing concept! This compelling, concise, slimmed-down Scripture is a must for anyone who finds those sixty-six books a tad daunting.'
Paul Kerensa, comedian and script writer

'A great introduction to the main stories in the Bible and it helps you to see how they fit together. It would be great to give as a gift.'
Five-star review on Amazon

The One Hour Bible
978 0 281 07964 3 • £4.99

 spck.org.uk /SPCKPublishing @SPCKPublishing  @SPCK_Publishing